Your Complete Guide To Party Entertaining

"You can stop worrying if you ever have to give or manage a party—turn to this book. It is, indeed, complete; the author even tells what to do with party-shy and other problem guests."

Book-of-the-Month Club News

"An excellent guide to entertaining. It gives specific and simple directions."

Louisville Courier-Journal

Party Fun and Games

former title: THE COMPLETE PARTY BOOK

by Alexander Van Rensselaer

A Crest Reprint

FAWCETT PUBLICATIONS, INC., GREENWICH, CONN.
MEMBER OF AMERICAN BOOK PUBLISHERS COUNCIL, INC.

PREFACE

THE THEME of this book is "fun for all, and all for fun." It is a book on how to have fun, whether with a small group of four or six persons, or with a big group of a dozen or more. Whether a couple of people drop in unexpectedly to pay their respects or you invite a crowd in for a good time, this book will tell you not only how to provide fun for your guests, but also how you can have fun doing so.

It simplifies the whole problem of entertaining; explains how to make people feel at home and at ease; how to provide amusement without making it seem that you have to turn the house upside down to do so; and how to lead everyone into enjoyable, cooperative activity without their being conscious of the fact that you are leading them.

Fun, to be real fun, should have the aura of spontaneity about it. This book will tell you how to make any kind of a party you wish to have seem so effortless that your guests will completely forget that they are being entertained and will participate with wholehearted enjoyment.

Here you will find a great variety of games, stunts, activities, and party plans to meet almost any situation or occasion.

This book describes in considerable detail a number of party plans for secular and religious holidays, birthdays, anniversaries, and so on. These plans are designed to serve as formulas which can be employed easily in devising many diversified types of parties. The formulas illustrated by the descriptions here can be successfully applied to almost any kind of a party one can think of: a Poverty Party, Ghost Party, Baseball Party, School Days Party, Hunter's Party, Wild Life Party, TV Party, or what have you.

In addition to the party plans, this book gives practical advice on how to prepare for a party, what kind of invitations to send and when to send them, how to serve different kinds of meals—including barbecues—in party fashion, and how to direct party pastimes and activities to keep the guests interested and amused. It also describes specifically and clearly the rules for a great many games, old and new, which are popular today with both young and old. All the suggestions given in this book have been tried and proven, and guarantee enjoyment.

"Throw" a party—and have fun!

A. Van R.

NEW YORK, 1956

Contents

CHAPTER   **PAGE**

‹ 1. WANT TO GIVE A PARTY?
    HERE'S HOW   11

    PROBLEMS TO BE CONSIDERED—
    INVITATIONS—PLANNING AND
    DIRECTING ACTIVITIES—PRIZES—
    WELCOMES AND INTRODUCTIONS—
    TABLE SEATING—FEEDING THE
    MULTITUDE—MOPPING UP

2. PARTY PLANS AND IDEAS   34

    HOLIDAY PARTIES—BIRTHDAY
    PARTIES—WEDDING ANNIVERSARY
    PARTIES

3. ACTIVE GAMES   71

4. DRAMATIC GAMES   118

5. ORAL GAMES   134

6. PAPER AND PENCIL GAMES   152

7. STUNTS   176

Party Fun
and Games

1. Want to Give a Party? Here's How

ARE YOU one of the hundreds of thousands who get the knee-quivers at the very thought of "throwing" a party; become panicky by the time the last guest has arrived, and the ice cream hasn't; develop battle fatigue before your party is half over; and collapse completely when you survey the chaos in your home after you have closed and locked the front door on the effusive thanks-for-a-simply-marvlus-time from the last couple who have overstayed their welcome?

It is strictly according to Hoyle for an otherwise intelligent, normal, healthy person to suffer a case of nerves, in one degree or another, on the eve of, during, or immediately after a party she or he has planned, launched, and navigated. But it really isn't necessary. Parties can be fun for everyone, including the host and hostess.

If you want to have fun, there are a few simple principles and practices for party-giving which will help you. They will reduce to a minimum the hazards which cause nerves, stage-fright, worry, and their like.

Take It Easy

The first rule of successful party-giving is, Relax; take it easy. More parties are ruined by the overanxiety of the host or hostess to do the thing up brown, to make his or her party the most original, and altogether the most memorable of parties held in the community.

These misguided entertainers overawe their guests at the very start with the elaborateness of the arrangements and decorations; chill the atmosphere with their officious and fussy directing; and scare the daylights out of everyone by their too obvious concern for the deportment of their guests and the safety of their household furnishings.

Generally speaking, the most successful parties, at which a really gay time is had by all, are those which are characterized by the simplicity of their decorations, activity programs, menus, and management, and are imbued with a genuine spirit of informality, friendliness, cooperation, and spontaneity.

An excellent principle, therefore, is, when planning a party, lean towards simplicity rather than elaborateness; and, when managing a party, avoid any semblance of nerve tension, rigid formality, regimentation, or just plain fussiness. Take it easy. Be yourself, and have a good time with your guests. It will pay dividends in fun.

This preliminary exhortation to simplicity does not mean that a successful party needs no advance planning and preparation. On the contrary, every party, large or small, formal or informal, should be thoughtfully planned and carefully prepared for ahead of time. But the primary purpose of what has previously been said is to impress upon the party-giver the fact that giving a party need not be an overburdensome, nerve-racking, and expensive undertaking. That is very important.

Problems To Be Considered

If you are going to give a party, here are some of the things to keep in mind.

First of all, why are you giving the party? To pay off

social obligations; to celebrate a special occasion, such as a birthday; or just to have a good time with some of your friends? The purpose of your party is important, because it will help you to decide what kind of a party to plan—a dance, a dinner, a luncheon, an evening of games, a card party, or whatever.

Another important consideration is the number of guests you intend to invite to your party. Some kinds of parties are adapted to large gatherings and others are especially designed for small intimate groups.

Then, if disaster is to be avoided, the space available for entertaining must be considered. You cannot very well hold a large wedding reception in a small two-room apartment. A bamboo tandem race wouldn't be much fun in an eighteen-by-fourteen-foot rumpus room. More people can be entertained at a buffet supper than can be entertained in the same available space at a formal dinner party. So the kind of party you will give and the number of people you will invite will depend on where you will do your entertaining.

Invitations

When you have decided upon the date of your party, the kind of a party it is to be, where it is to be held, and the persons you wish to attend, the next thing is to design and send out the invitations. Suggestions for informal invitations to special parties are given elsewhere in this book. If the party is to be formal, with traditional evening dress required, your invitations should follow the customary form, with no embellishments—

Mr. and Mrs. A. B. Seabee
request the pleasure of your company
at a dinner and dance
to be held on
July 4, 19—
at the Sailon Yacht Club
Bluenose, Backneck, New York
at eight o'clock in the evening

R.S.V.P.

It is not strictly required that such formal invitations be engraved. It is acceptable to have them printed (some printing processes are not easily distinguishable from engraving), or even neatly handwritten on formal stationery. The wording and its arrangement on the card or letterpaper indicate the formality of the occasion. Of course, for very special occasions, such as a wedding or a large ball, to which a great many people are to be invited, an engraved invitation is preferable.

For such parties invitations should be mailed well in advance of the date of the party—three or four weeks—so that you will know how many acceptances there are in ample time to arrange for the catering, etc., and so that those you invite may know of your plans before they have accepted other invitations for the same day.

But this book is interested only in less formal affairs, at which playing games or informal dancing will be the chief interest. Such parties can be very elaborate, as, for instance, those which call for special costumes, buffet suppers, unusual decorations, and a considerable amount of planning.

In the case of more informal parties, invitations need not be mailed more than one to two weeks ahead of time, depending on how large the party is to be. If you are to have a small card party, or a dessert-and-coffee shindig, for ten or a dozen of your friends, you could dispatch the invitations a week or ten days before.

Invitations for informal parties offer talented and witty hostesses a wide range of opportunities for creating artistic or amusing cards, cutouts, notes, etc., which will be welcomed and often treasured by those who receive them. But be warned not to be too ambitious. Poetry is for poets to make, and rhymes are for rhymesters. If you have a flare for either, by all means, when the occasion is appropriate, write your invitation in poetry or rhyme. For those who are not so talented, it is safer to write the invitation in sincere, straightforward prose, on a plain white card or on your personal notepaper, with, perhaps, a comic sketch or a cutout added for decoration.

This sort of thing—

Dear Sue,
Peter and I are celebrating our tenth anniversary on June 12, with an informal party at our house, from 6:30 on, in the evening, and we want very much to have you and George with us. We hope you will answer yes.

Mary Winks

is a good deal better than an insipid effort, such as—

On the anniversary of our wedding,
We are having a party to celebrate.
At six-thirty o'clock, on June the twelfth,
Come to our igloo, and don't be late.
Mary and Peter Winks

Planning and Directing Activities

More will be said about invitations later. The next step in preparing for your party is to plan what you will do at the party to entertain your guests. Detailed suggestions for entertaining at various types of parties will be found in another section of this book; but there are certain general principles of entertaining which apply to every party, of whatever kind, and these you should know.

You cannot please all of the people all of the time. Human nature being what it is, there are differences of taste and interests in every group, large or small. Therefore, in planning party activities, think of the likes and dislikes of the persons who are coming to the party, and try to have a sufficient variety in your entertainment program, so that each guest will find at least one thing on the program that will be to his liking. If you know your guests well, this will not be difficult.

A very common mistake is to include in a party program activities that will put certain guests "on the spot," demanding of them individual performances of feats which, for one reason or another, they are quite incapable of doing. A person whose mind goes blank every time he is expected in public to give an oral answer to a brain-teaser, or information-please question, should not have such a question thrown at him. A tone-deaf person should not be asked to sing a solo, for any reason. In general, team games, and stunts in which two or more persons can participate at the same time, are more successful as entertainment than games and stunts which put the individual guests on their own. The combined intelligence or skill of a team overshadows the failings of any of its members.

In planning your program, be sure to include some activity for the early birds. It is unusual for all the guests to arrive at a party at the same time. Unless you have planned something to keep the early arrivals occupied while waiting for the latecomers, there will be an awkward half-hour or so of strained conversation and impatient fidgeting.

Also in your program you should include a few extra specialties, or stunts, or surprises to be held in reserve for introduction in emergencies. If a brain-teaser game, for instance, is beginning to drag, you can stop it, and draw from your reserve a pastime of quite a different nature, and immediately substitute it for the brain-teaser game.

There is another secret of successful party management. Once your party has started, keep it moving. The instant you become aware of a fading interest in a game or other pastime, immediately introduce a new activity. Most games will hold the players' interest only for a relatively short time, 20 to 30 minutes. A safe rule to follow is, when the interest and enthusiasm of the players in a game have reached its peak, stop that particular game and start another. It is a great temptation, when a game is going particularly well, to prolong it, or repeat it again and again. This is a mistake. If it is stopped at the moment of most enjoyment, it will be remembered by the players as one of the best games they ever played; whereas, if it is continued or repeated, interest in it is

16

almost certain to diminish, and the players will quickly become restless and disappointed.

Regimentation was referred to earlier in this chapter. No one anywhere, least of all at a party, enjoys being bossed, pushed around, or continually told what to do. So the hostess should take care not to overdo the directing of her party. Her rôle should be that of a leader, rather than of a drill sergeant. It is a good procedure to ask different guests, from time to time, to help in arranging the furniture for different pastimes, serving the refreshments, scoring and judging contests, and so on. To do this will please your guests, make you less conspicuous as the boss, and give the guests the feeling that they have had a share in making the party a success.

Another way to avoid the stigma of regimentation is to plan your activity program so that there will be occasional "breathing spells" between different groups of activities. These intermissions should not be prolonged, but should give the guests enough time to intermingle and form new groupings for the next activity.

One more pointer on supervising games should be mentioned. Some games call for the elimination of players while the game is in progress. "Ghosts" is customarily played that way. This, however, is rarely satisfactory. The first few to be eliminated usually become thoroughly bored waiting on the sidelines for the game to end. A better method is to score a point against the failing player and let him continue in the game.

Before a game or activity is begun, be sure that every participant clearly understands what is to be expected of him. Do not take for granted that everyone is familiar with all the activities you have chosen for your program. There are many variations in the procedures of almost every game, and, if the procedures you wish to have followed are not understood by the players, confusion and argumentation will result.

When you introduce a pastime, describe what happens, and then ask for questions, to clear up doubtful points. In some cases, you can have a few persons who know the pastime give a brief demonstration.

17

Prizes

The matter of prizes and scoring is a matter that needs thoughtful consideration. Everyone likes to receive a reward of one kind or another for a superior achievement. On the other hand, it is very disappointing to some persons to leave empty-handed a party where prizes have been awarded.

As you are undoubtedly well aware, some persons take their games seriously, often too seriously for the good of an informal party. Others play simply for the fun of it, and try to help with the fun as much as they can. A few play indifferently, just for the sake of the company —to be one of the gang. Under such circumstances there is no good in trying to put party pastimes on the level of professional competition and award prizes. It just can't be done without offending some one.

If prizes are to be given, they should be distributed in a spirit of fun, as part of the entertainment, and should be of little value excepting for their comical nature or aptness.

One way to make the distribution of the prizes a part of the entertainment is to adopt a point scoring system for each of the party activities, and instruct each guest to keep a record of the points he accumulates during the party. At the end of the party, a table or tray is brought in, on which are the prizes, daintily gift-wrapped, as many as you care to provide. These prizes are then auctioned off, unopened, the guests bidding for them with the points they have scored previously. This is fun in itself, and makes a very pleasant and jolly concluding pastime.

In awarding point scores, every member of a winning team should receive 5 points. In other games, where each player is on his own, and there is only one winner, the winner alone gets 10 points. In games such as Wink (#51), a scoring method is suggested in this book for each game.

When the accumulative scoring method is used, each guest should be provided with a tally card on which to keep a record of his score.

Prizes are most suitable for special parties, at which most of the time is devoted to one pastime, such as bridge or an outdoor treasure hunt.

In selecting prizes, you need not be concerned over their monetary value. There are many inexpensive articles that make very welcomed prizes—playing cards, cigarettes, handkerchiefs, address books, packs of matches, a package of razor blades, facial tissue, powder puffs, etc. Original and comic prizes are best of all, such things as can be purchased inexpensively in novelty shops—puzzles, tricks, joke books, gadgets, etc. "White elephants" about your house also make acceptable, and often amusing prizes.

Welcomes and Introductions

Be sure to have everything, including yourself, in readiness for your party well before party time, so that the early guests will be spared the embarrassment of arriving ahead of the hostess. Although you may be sure that most of your guests will arrive a little after the time stated in your invitation, there are always a few punctilious souls who make it a fetish to be strictly on time, or just a bit before time, and they should not be penalized for their promptness by being made to feel uncomfortable.

As you welcome each arrival, tell him where to leave his or her wraps. At small, informal parties, the host may take both the ladies' and gentlemen's wraps, and hang them in a closet, or place them in a room reserved for the purpose. At larger parties, one "cloak room" should be reserved for the ladies and another for the gentlemen; and the hostess simply directs the guests, as they arrive, to one or the other of these rooms.

If your party is large and among your guests are a number of persons who are unknown to the others, it is unnecessary for you to attempt to introduce them to each other and to everyone else in the room. All that is required is for you to introduce each stranger to one or two of the other guests and let him carry on for himself from there. A number of ice-breaking games are suggested in this book which have been designed to make it easy for the guests to get to know each other.

When, during the course of a party, you spy an outlander hiding back of a chair or in a corner, because he thinks he is not being accepted as one of the crowd, it will be necessary for you to take him in hand and reorientate him by introducing him to some kindly, carefree soul whom he may not have yet met; ask him to do some chore for you, such as passing cigarettes or refreshments; or steering him into a group competition or conversation. Nothing is more deadening to the spirit of a party than a shy outsider who feels he is not wanted. Any one showing the slightest indication of such a feeling must be attended to immediately, both for his own good and for the good of the party.

In small parties where there are only one or two strangers present, it is best to introduce each in turn to all the other guests.

The rules governing introductions are very simple. The man is presented to the lady, rarely the lady to the man, unless the man be a dignitary or is old enough to be the lady's grandfather: youth is presented to age. The presentation speech should be brief, unadorned, and sincere. When you introduce one of your personal friends to another personal friend, you may say: "Helena, I'd like to introduce my good friend, Henry Adam. Henry, this is Helena Hellona." That is all there is to it. The "Mister," "Miss," "Mrs.," or any other title need only be used on very formal occasions, or when you are introducing a casual acquaintance; some one you have only very recently met; a young person to a considerably older person; or just an ordinary guy to a really big shot.

It is a great help at a party, if, when you are bringing two persons together for the first time, you can say something personal about each, after the introduction. In the case of Helena Hellona and Henry Adams, you might say to Helena, "Henry is a tennis enthusiast"; and to Henry you might say, "Helena is crazy about horses." Immediately Helena and Henry have something to talk about, and so won't have to comment on the weather.

Table Seating

Table seating is always something of a problem, especially so when you are entertaining a large number of persons. Care must be taken to see that the wrong people do not sit next to each other. In general, arrange the seating so that the guests are well mixed. Husbands and wives should be separated, they have opportunity enough at home for conversation; the girl and her heavy boy friend should not be placed together, otherwise no one else at the table will hear from them; place the good conversationalists on opposite sides of the table, so as to spread their conversation for the benefit of all; seat the shy girl next to a gay fellow who won't let her coyness scare him; and the stranger, known only to the host and hostess, should be placed within easy voice range of either the host or hostess, or next to some one who has previously expressed an interest in meeting him or her. When there is a guest of honor, he sits at the right of the hostess, if a man; and she sits at the right of the host, if a lady.

The seating arrangement should be planned for the purpose of stimulating general conversation at the table and for providing good fun for every one.

Feeding the Multitude

What, when, and how to feed your guests is not such a frightening challenge as some hostesses make it appear to be.

The clever hostess will select for her menu simple dishes which can be prepared well ahead of party time and need only to be reheated just before serving time, or served cold. She will not attempt to prepare elaborate dishes which, if they don't require her undivided attention in the kitchen, will at best keep her on the run from the living room to the kitchen and back, to the distraction and discomfort of the guests. Plan your meals so that all the heavy work will be behind you by party time, when you will want to greet your guests and entertain them without interruption.

After all, nourishment is by all odds the least important feature of party entertaining, although, of course, it has its place. But, as a famous wit suggested, when he said to his hostess, "A fig for your bill-of-fare, give me a bill of your company," the really important elements of a party are good fellowship and merry-making. If you keep your guests interested and amused, they will not be critical of your bill-of-fare.

That does not mean that your meal or refreshments may be uninteresting or unattractively served. On the contrary, you should put your originality and ingenuity to work, and try to dress up your dishes to the best advantage. When possible, at least one dish on the menu should be something out of the ordinary. Many a familiar dish can be wonderfully disguised by the addition of this or that, and made to look most appetizing by the manner in which it is garnished and served.

What, When, and How

When and how to serve the victuals depends on the kind of party you are giving.

Brunch is a combination of breakfast and luncheon, and can be served any time before noon. It should be a very informal, intimate, more or less self-service affair, enjoyed most when it is served, in cold weather, on tables set before the open hearth in the living room, or, in warm weather, on the porch or terrace, or in the garden. It should be a fairly substantial meal, such as fruit juice or grapefruit; eggs; cream chicken and waffles; toast, muffins, or hotcakes; preserves; and coffee—plenty of coffee.

Luncheons are usually served very informally about one o'clock on a table that is covered with pretty place mats or colorful peasant linen, with a low centerpiece of daintily arranged flowers or fruits. Candles are omitted, and white table linen is never used. The luncheon menu should be very simple, and may consist of only one course: toasted cheese sandwiches, fruit salad, and tea or coffee. For a three-course luncheon you could serve tomato juice, fruit juice, or soup (hot in winter; cold or jellied in the summer); stuffed peppers, lamb chops, or creamed chicken; green salad; ice cream or sherbert; tea or coffee; hot bread or Melba toast.

The serving routine for a luncheon is not complicated. The table is set, with service plates at each place and the accoutrements where they should be. These will include the silver, the coffee cups and saucers, the tumblers, the bread plates, the filled sugar bowl, the filled cream pitcher, the small silver, glass, or china dishes filled with nuts and candies, and so on.

If it is a one-course luncheon, the hostess, as soon as the guests are seated, brings in from the kitchen, one at a time, the luncheon plates, which have been filled in the kitchen, and substitutes them for the service plates on the table, serving each guest from the left. She then brings in the hot bread, muffins, toast, or whatever is intended, and asks one of the guests to help herself and pass the serving plate on to the next guest. She brings in the coffee and fills each cup, allowing the guests to help themselves to the cream and sugar, if they wish either or both.

If a three-course luncheon is served, the tomato juice, brought in on a tray, may be served in the living room as soon as the guests have arrived. Fruit cups, or cold soup, are placed on the service plates on the table just before the luncheon is served. Hot soup is brought in and placed on the service plates after the guests are seated at the table. The service plates are removed with the fruit cup, cold soup service, or hot soup service, and the luncheon plates, filled in the kitchen, are brought in and put in place, serving from the left as usual. After the main course has been finished, the empty luncheon plates are removed two at a time, and the dessert, individually served in the kitchen, or previously arranged in individual servings, is brought in and properly placed. The hostess then brings in and serves the coffee, the guests helping themselves to the cream, sugar, bonbons, nuts, etc.

Afternoon tea is served any time after three; usually from four to six o'clock. It is probably most often served after an afternoon of bridge, a meeting of the literary club or sewing circle, or any other social or sports activity.

The tea is served from a tray placed on a low table in the living room, on the porch or terrace, or in the garden. On the tray are the tea service, with sugar bowl, cream pitcher, a small dish covered with slices of lemons, the tea cups and saucers, small tea plates, the silver, and an adequate supply of small napkins, either linen or paper. Sandwiches, cookies, and other foods, if any, are brought in on trays and placed on a nearby table.

The hostess places the tea cup and its saucer on one of the small tea plates, and makes the tea according to the preference of the guest, with or without sugar and with either cream or lemon. She places a spoon and one of the small napkins beside the cup and passes the entire arrangement to the guest. The guests help themselves to the food, passing the serving plates from one to another. Beverages other than tea are frequently served at tea parties: lemonade, orangeade, ginger ale, etc.

The *formal dinner* is no longer what it used to be in the days when there was no servant problem and food was relatively inexpensive. In those days a twelve-course dinner was by no means the exception. The menu for such a dinner would consist of (1) Canapes, oysters, or clams, (2) soup, (3) fish, (4) an entrée, (5) asparagus or artichokes, (6) a joint with one vegetable and potato, (7) frozen punch, omelet, or soufflé, (8) game or poultry and salad, (9) sweet pudding or Bavarian cream, (10) frozen dessert and individual cakes, (11) fruit and bon-bons, and (12) coffee. More frequently the entrée, the vegetable, and the frozen punch courses were omitted, and sometimes the game or poultry course also.

Although such elaborate dinners are still served at banquets and on very special occasions when the services of a professional caterer are employed, the customary formal dinner served in the home today is a much simpler undertaking. An adequate menu for a formal dinner served at home would be (1) oysters, clams, or grapefruit, (2) soup, (3) a roast with one vegetable and potato, (4) salad, (5) dessert, and (6) coffee, served in the living room.

The formal dinner, even in its present-day simplified form and, so often, maidless service, requires painstaking planning and preparation.

Formal dinners today are given only on special occasions, to celebrate a birthday or wedding anniversary, before a formal dance, to announce an engagement, etc.

For the formal dinner the table should be elegantly set with your very best linen, china, glass, and silver. The centerpiece and other floral decorations should be as lovely as you can arrange them. The centerpiece must not be so high as to prevent the guests from seeing each other across the table, and the candles should be over head-high, so that they will not flicker annoyingly in the eyes of the guests. Place cards are not required unless more than ten guests are expected; the hostess simply tells each guest where he or she is to sit.

When you are entertaining without the help of a maid, the best plan is to follow the family style of service, where all the food is served at the table by the host and hostess, rather than brought from the kitchen in individual servings. The oysters or grapefruit are placed on the table just before dinner is announced. The soup is served by the hostess, and the meat carved and served by the host. The vegetables are placed on the table and each guest in turn serves himself. The salad is also placed on the table and served by the host, who may or may not mix the dressing at the table, as he wishes. The dessert is served by the hostess. Coffee is served in the living room by the hostess.

Serving the food and removing the empty plates should be done with the least possible confusion. A tea wagon is a great convenience. It is placed beside the hostess's chair, and after each course the empty plates are passed to her, one by one, and she places them on the lower shelf of the wagon, and then quietly wheels the wagon to the kitchen where the soiled plates are removed and the materials for the next course are arranged on the top shelf of the wagon.

To avoid confusion, only the hostess or another member of the family should bring things to and from the kitchen.

Arrange the seating so that the hostess, if she is to serve, sits at the end of the table nearest the entrance to the kitchen, with the male guest of honor on her right. The host sits at the opposite end of the table, with the female guest of honor on his right. If another member of the family is to serve, he or she is placed near the kitchen.

The time for a formal dinner depends on the after-dinner program. If the dinner precedes an evening of bridge, games, dancing, or just pleasant conversation, it may be served as late as eight o'clock.

The *informal dinner,* or "company dinner," is becoming more and more popular, and is rapidly displacing the formal dinner. The informal dinner differs from the formal dinner in that the guests are not expected to wear formal attire and all ceremonious procedures are abandoned and the atmosphere is that of freedom from restraints, and relaxation. But that does not mean that the informal dinner should not be given just as much thought and attention in planning and serving as a formal dinner. It means only that the arrangements are much simpler, the table much less elaborately arrayed, and the menu need have no more than three or four courses. The menu for an informal dinner might be soup or fruit cocktail, a meat course with vegetable and potato, salad, dessert, and coffee.

The table setting for an informal dinner should be pleasing and pretty, but not showy. A white linen table-cloth and linen napkins may be used, but pretty colored table linen is now just as acceptable. A centerpiece of appropriate flowers attractively arranged and two or four tall candles will add charm to the table setting.

A serving plate is placed at each place at the table and on either side of it the silver which will be needed for the meal. A tumbler, for water, is placed above and to the right of the serving plate, at the tip of the knife, and the bread and butter plate to the left of the serving plate at the tip of the fork. The butter knife is placed on the bread and butter plate parallel with the edge of the table. Just before dinner is served a pat of butter is placed on each bread and butter plate, each tumbler

26

is three-quarters filled with water, and the candles are lighted. If jelly or relishes are to be served they are placed on the table at this time in small silver, glass, or china dishes. If the first course is grapefruit, fruit cup, or jellied soup, it is placed on the serving plates now. Hot soup is not served until the guests are seated.

Coffee is most enjoyed when served after the meal, in the living room. The coffee may be poured in the kitchen and the small cups on their saucers, each with a small coffee spoon placed on the saucer with its handle parallel with the handle of the cup and pointing to the right, are brought in on a tray, on which also are placed a full cream pitcher and a full sugar bowl. Each guest helps himself to the coffee as it is passed around by the hostess and takes what cream and sugar he wishes.

If she so desires, the hostess may bring the coffee service into the living room and place it on a low table, from which she serves the coffee individually, asking each guest in turn what are his or her wishes regarding sugar and cream.

The *buffet meal* is the ideal method of entertaining a large number of people without the services of a maid. The buffet meal may be served at any hour, and may be formal or informal. It is a self-service affair; all the food being temptingly arranged on one table, with all the necessary accoutrements. The kind of food placed on the table depends on the kind of meal that is served— breakfast, brunch, luncheon, evening collation, supper, or whatever it may be.

In buffet service the important thing is the arrangement of the serving table, which must be the center of attraction. The table should be covered with a linen tablecloth and have on it lovely flowers and greens, artistically arranged. The table setting will depend on the food to be served. In general, the heartiest foods are placed at the ends of the table, the salads in between with the sandwiches, nuts, celery, olives, etc. The plates required are stacked on the table and the silver, forks and spoons, are arranged in rows near them. The napkins, overlapping one another, are placed in neat rows.

If hot food is to be served, or meat to be carved, you

may ask one or two of your friends to attend to this. As each guest enters the dining room he goes to the buffet serving table and receives from whoever is serving a plate with the meat, or whatever it may be, on it. He then circulates around the table and helps himself to vegetables, salad, rolls, sandwiches, celery, or whatever he wishes to select from what is available. Finally, he picks up a knife and fork and napkin. At the end of this course, the table is cleared and the dessert and coffee service brought in. The dessert plates and spoons, and the coffee cups, saucers, and spoons may have been included in the original table setting and should be left when the table is cleared. Otherwise they are brought in with the dessert and coffee service. The guests leave their soiled first-course plates on a side table or other small tables provided for the purpose; and return to the buffet serving table, where they serve themselves with the dessert and coffee. The hostess and those she has asked to assist her remove as quickly as possible the soiled plates.

At a buffet meal it is customary for the men to serve the ladies and then serve themselves. As many chairs, sofas, and small tables as are available should be arranged along the sides of the living room and other rooms for the ladies to sit in while they eat. At a formal buffet meal, small tables, such as card tables, seating four persons, may be set up in the dining room, living room, and elsewhere, and two couples sit at each table, the men obtaining and serving the food. Each table should be covered with a cloth and have on it a small vase with three or four roses, or other flowers, in it; a lighted candle; and an ashtray, with matches and a package of cigarettes on it.

Late evening *snacks* are served after an evening's entertainment. Invite your friends in on the way home from the movies, or ice skating, or a party at some other house, and without any formality, give them a "bite," which may be anything from gingerale and crackers to welsh rarebit, or grilled hamburgers, with a salad, dessert, and coffee. Snacks may be served in the kitchen, at the dining-room table, or "lap" style in the living room before a cheerfully crackling open fire, in the winter, or on the porch, in summer. The hostess may bring the snacks in on a big tray, have them all in readiness on the dining-room table, or serve them right off the stove in the kitchen. The hour of snacks is one of the pleasantest forms of entertaining. It is an hour of complete relaxation and amusing conversation. Anything goes, so long as it is within the bounds of common decency. The conversation is personal, but never unkindly, and focuses on the previous events and activities of the day and evening. Anecdotes are told and stories repeated. After the snacks have been consumed, the guests may, and often do, help with the tidying-up, before going home.

Dessert meals offer a delightful way to entertain informally and are becoming more and more popular in the servantless house. The guests are invited to come after luncheon, dinner, or supper for *dessert and coffee*, and to remain for cards, games, television, dancing, or just stimulating conversation and good fellowship. The dessert and coffee are served buffet style from the dining-room table, which should be covered with a pretty linen cloth and attractively decorated and set. The dessert should be something out of the ordinary, accompanied with plenty of small cakes, nuts, candy, and coffee. The guests find everything they need, plates, spoons, cups and saucers, etc., arranged on the table, and help themselves to whatever they want.

Perhaps the most popular type of party in the United States today is a *barbecue*. Its advantages are that it is adaptable to almost any occasion and to the entertaining of any number of persons.

The word barbecue probably comes from the Haitian word barbacoa, which means a framework of sticks set upon posts, frequently employed for the drying or curing of fish and meat over an open fire. In the south and southwest of the United States a barbecue came to mean a large social or political entertainment at which animals are roasted whole over an open fire as part of a sumptuous feast. Recently the term barbecue has been applied to almost any meal at which is served roast, broiled, or grilled meats, prepared over a charcoal or hickory fire, and usually outdoors.

The best barbecue parties are held on a porch, in the backyard or patio, or on a penthouse or apartment terrace. The cooking is done over an outdoor fireplace or over one of the many varieties of portable grills or smoker-braziers which are now available within the price range of all. The menu for a barbecue may be as simple as charcoal-broiled hamburgers (or frankfurters) between rolls, roast corn-on-the-cob, tossed salad, apple pie, and coffee. Or it may be as elaborate as you wish, including steaks, pork chops, chicken, and the like with rich, spicy barbecue sauces, garlic bread, etc.

Barbecue parties are almost always informal, and rightly so. Bluejeans, shorts, and other types of sports clothes are more appropriate for open-fire cooking and picnic-style eating than evening gowns and dress shirts.

Colored lights, Japanese lanterns, or other types of illumination should be used around your porch, yard, patio, or terrace to create an atmosphere of warmth and cheerfulness. Colorful paper plates and cups will contribute more to the gaiety of the scene than china and glass, will be much easier to handle, and will eliminate the chore of dishwashing.

Entertaining the guests at a barbecue is a simple matter. A barbecue should be pretty much of a cooperative affair. Everybody should be invited and encouraged to help with the preparation of the feast, which should be conducted on a self-service basis; and they should also be encouraged to help with the cleaning up.

After the meal is over and everything has been cleared away, the most appropriate pastime for the guests is perhaps square dancing, which may be participated in to the accompaniment of a record player.

The *Cocktail hour* offers, perhaps, the easiest, certainly the most convivial, way of entertaining. The best time for this jolly form of sociality is between four and seven o'clock in the late afternoon. Invitations are usually issued over the telephone, anywhere from one to ten days ahead of time.

When only a few people have been invited, not more than a dozen or fourteen, cocktails are served; when more than fourteen are expected, it is more convenient, and just as much fun, to serve punch. The cocktails and punch may be non-alcoholic or alcoholic, according to your own taste. If cocktails are served, a choice of cocktails should be offered the guests—say, tomato juice, grapefruit juice, grape juice, or one of the colas. If you serve alcoholic cocktails, be sure to have available tomato juice cocktails, or one of the colas, for those who prefer not to drink alcoholic beverages. They will be appreciated, and will relieve the non-alcoholic drinking guest of the feeling of non-participation in the festivities.

At a small cocktail party, the host brings in the cocktails on a tray and serves them, refilling the glasses later from the cocktail shaker or a pitcher, depending on the kind of cocktails served. If tall drinks are served—highballs, gingerale, ades, or colas—the glasses are neatly arranged on a table, with a large bowl of cracked ice and the bottles containing the beverage (or the pitcher containing the ade). The beverage bottles should be brought in from the icebox and placed on the table as needed, so that they will have no chance of getting warm. They are opened and served at the table, and the filled glasses are passed, on a tray, to the guests.

The hostess provides each guest with a cocktail napkin, and serves the hors d'oeuvres.

At large cocktail parties, the service is buffet style, the beverages served from a table at one end of the room and the hors d'oeuvres from another table across the room. This encourages the guests to circulate and hobnob with each other in passing from the beverage table to the food table.

Don't let the hors d'oeuvres problem worry you. Cocktails are served just before the dining hour, and your guests will not thank you for tempting them to destroy their appetites by offering them a great variety of fancy canapes, hors d'oeuvres, and sandwiches that are as nourishing as they are irresistible. A few dainty, open sandwiches make a pretty display on the hors d'oeuvres table, when accompanied by attractively arranged bowls and dishes of potato chips, long thin slices of carrots, florets of cauliflower, radishes cut rose shape, stuffed

31

celery, stuffed olive, and cheese and mayonnaise dips and dressings. The vegetables should be thoroughly chilled and served very cold.

The hors d'oeuvres table should be covered with a linen cloth, and set with a pretty centerpiece; silver, glass, or china plates for the hors d'oeuvres; and cocktail napkins; but no flat silver.

The beverage table should be covered with a linen cloth and set with the needed glassware, cracked-ice bowl, and whatever else will be used in serving the beverage. If punch is served, the punch bowl should be the center of attention and be as attractive as possible in appearance. Stand a block of ice in the bowl a short time before the party to chill the bowl thoroughly. At party time pour in the punch, filling about two thirds of the bowl. As the punch is consumed, replenish the supply. The guests are expected to help themselves to the punch, as well as to the hors d'oeuvres.

Be sure to have plenty of ash trays distributed around the rooms which will be used by the guests, and see that they are frequently emptied during the party.

Mopping Up

So far we have been concerned with organizing and directing a party. Now we come to the sixty-four thousand-dollar problem—how to get rid of the never-say-die guests and reconvert your dwelling to normal use again.

If you are giving a small, informal dinner party for six or eight intimate friends, it is quite all right to have the washing up and putting away of the used plates and silver as one of your party activities. Many hands make light work. Not only that, many a good time has been had in a friend's kitchen, helping with the washing-up, assisted by a half-a-dozen other friends.

Of course, if you are entertaining a large number of guests, you can't very well ask every one to stay around and do the housecleaning for you, after the party is over. The best plan is to stack all the used dishes, etc., in the kitchen, and tackle as many of them as you have strength to manage immediately after the last guest has gone, leaving the rest, and the housecleaning, until the morning. And here is a word to the wise: the more you are able to clean up right after a party, the less you are going to regret the party the next day. There is nothing more detrimental to your morale than viewing on the next morning the leftovers of the party of the night before.

The guest who has had a wonderful time and who hates to say goodbye, is probably the most difficult problem. And, if you have done a really good job as host or hostess, you will have on your hands more than one guest who will have the urge to linger. The best way to handle these delinquents is to put them to work. Say to one, "Oh, George, would you mind just emptying those ashtrays, before you go?" And to another say, "You'll be a dear, if, before you leave, you will just help me put these chairs back where they belong." Go right about your business of cleaning up, and, one by one, the late-stayers will drift off; but not until they have helped you considerably in straightening things up. If any one is persistent enough to stay until the last chair has been put back in place and the last teaspoon has been washed and put away, all you can do is be honest, and say, "You have been perfectly wonderful, and I don't know how to thank you for all you have done to help make my party a success. Thank you ever so much. Good night. I am going to turn in." If, after that, the guest still lingers, there is only one of two things left for you to do: make up a bed on the couch in the living room, and let him spend the night there; or shove him out the front door, and lock the door after him.

2. *Party Plans and Ideas*

As HAS already been said, parties should be carefully planned. The planning should include the activity program, as well as the time, place, number of guests, decorations, and menu.

In planning the activity program, consider first your guests and what is likely to amuse them. But, remember, no matter how hard you try to anticipate the interests and moods of your guests, you will not always be successful. Therefore, your program should be flexible, and you should be prepared to make changes in it, if the occasion demands. Many a party has been ruined because the hostess has planned a program and has stuck to it from beginning to end, in spite of everything. If your guests have arrived in the mood for rug-cutting and high-jinks, please do not present them with pencils and paper, and require them to answer twenty questions on current affairs! By all means let them dance; but keep your eye on them, and the minute you see that an appreciable number of them are beginning to lose interest in the rug-cutting, suggest one of the activities you had originally planned, and go on from there.

The following party plans are purposely not worked out in great detail. Your decorations, for example, will depend upon what you have at hand and what you are able and can afford to procure. The purpose of the plans is only to suggest ways and means by which you can have fun entertaining your friends on various occasions. These plans are adaptable to large and small gatherings. All of them have been successful with mixed groups of adults.

34

Holiday Parties

Traditional religious holidays have long been occasions for parties; and, because of the customs associated with them, they make party planning relatively simple. Decorations, table favors, games, and menus are suggested by the things which tradition has so closely connected with these special days.

Twelfth Night

Twelfth-Night, or the eve of Twelfth-Day (the twelfth day after Christmas), which is also called Old Christmas, was for a great many years generally observed as a popular and domestic holiday, and was celebrated in many places with great pomp, pageantry, and noise. It was the custom on this night to have a feast at which the Twelfth-cake, or bean cake, "that beautiful, frosted, festooned, bedizened, and ornamental piece of confectionery," was served. In this cake were imbedded a bean and a pea (or a ring). The persons finding the bean and the pea in their servings of the cake became King and Queen of Twelfth-Night. Three hundred years ago the ingredients of the bean cake, we are told, were flour, honey, ginger, and pepper.

It was also the custom on this occasion to sketch or paint on cards pictoral representations of grotesque Twelfth-Night characters. Each guest took one of these cards, from a "grab bag," and for the duration of the festivities wore it on his sleeve. Nathan B. Warren wrote in his *The Holidays* (1876): "In London, it is or was the custom for the Lord Mayor to give a Twelfth-Night party at the Mansion House. The King and Queen of the Bean were chosen by lot, and were surrounded not by 'baboons, apes, and other wild animals,' but by highly respectable ladies and gentlemen who wore pictoral representations of grotesque Twelfth-Night characters, which they were expected to sustain."

Frequently a Court Fool was also chosen by lot at these Twelfth-Night festivities, and he was expected to play the part throughout the evening.

At a modern Twelfth-Night party the bean-cake should be the center of attraction at the supper or refreshment table. It should be gaily decorated and on it should stand a doll king and queen. Room decorations, of course, will be the same as for Christmas, a tinsel-bedecked and lighted Christmas tree, evergreens, etc. Paper crowns and a fool's cap should be provided for the Bean King and Queen and the Court Fool.

The pastimes should consist of cutting and passing the cake to discover the King and Queen; drawing the pictoral cards from the grab bag; choosing the Court Fool by lot; crowning the King and Queen; and holding court.

Holding court is managed in this way.

All of the guests excepting the King, Queen, and Fool retire to an adjoining room. The King, Queen, and Fool then arrange the throne. At one end of the room they place three straight-backed chairs in a row, side by each. Then they remove the center chair and put in its place, on the floor, a large, soft sofa-cushion, or pillow. Across the seats of the remaining chairs, and over the pillow, they stretch a strip of canvas, or other strong fabric, which should be long enough to lap over the sides of the chairs, and wide enough to cover the chair seats. This entire arrangement is then covered with drapery in such a way as to make it appear as a single, armless settee. The drapery must completely hide the chairs and the cushion.

The King and Queen now seat themselves on the two chairs and the Fool gaily brings in from the adjoining room one guest at a time to be presented at Court. He announces the guest as Lady so-and-so or the Duke of this-or-that, and leads the guest to the throne, where she, or he, after making a courtly curtsy or bow, kneels before the royalty, and solemnly says, "Your Highnesses; your humble servant." The King then says: "Arise, my humble servant and be seated," and points to the vacant space between himself and the Queen. As the humble servant sits down, the King and Queen, with great dignity, arise. The humble servant sits, sans dignity.

The humble servant is then assisted to his, or her, feet,

36

the throne is rearranged, and the Fool gaily brings in the next victim.

Other pastimes for a Twelfth-Night Party are (1) to have each guest represent in pantomime the creature pictured on his card; (2) Blind Man's Buff (#6); (3) Slap Jack (#40), and (4) Who Is Your Neighbor? (#49).

The most fitting end to a Twelfth-Night Party would be for every one to gather around the piano and sing Christmas carols.

Pancake Tuesday

Who hasn't heard of Mardi Gras, Pancake Tuesday, Fasterns' E'en, or Shrove Tuesday? They were, until very recent times, all one and the same thing—the day before the first day of Lent; a day of special merrymaking and revelry. In bygone times this day was an occasion for hilarity, mummeries, games, tricks, masques, pageants, and spectacular processions. It was also the day on which the pancake or flapjack came into its own.

On this day it was, and in many places still is, customary to serve pancakes. An early seventeenth-century description of Pancake Tuesday says: "There is a thing cal'd wheaten flowre, which the cookes doe mingle with water, egges, spice, and other tragicall, magicall inchantments, and then put it little by little into a frying pan of boyling suet, where it makes a confused dismall hissing until, at last, by the skill of the cooke, it is transformed into the form of a flap-jack, cal'd a Pancake, which ominous incantation the ignorant people doe devoure very greedily."

If you want to have fun, give a pancake party on Pancake (Shrove) Tuesday. Make it a dessert-and-coffee party, inviting your guests to come after their supper. Serve the pancakes hot off the griddle, and, after the pancakes, serve plenty of hot coffee.

After your guests have had their fill of pancakes and coffee, play the Bell Game, an adaptation of an ancient Shrove-Tuesday game called Threshing the Fat Hen.

The Bell Game is played in this manner. Blindfold all

the players but one, and place in the hand of each blindfolded player a light switch or a rolled-up newspaper. Around the neck of the player who is not blindfolded hang two or three bells. At the signal to begin, "It," the player with the bells, dodges about the room, trying to avoid the other players, while the other players follow the sound of the bells and try to strike It with their switches. When It is struck by a player, he immediately takes his bells from his neck and drops them on the floor. The player who struck him must quickly hand him his blindfold and switch and then pick up the bells. This player then becomes It, and the player who was struck joins in the chase, after being blindfolded.

It was the custom on this day for the mummers to burlesque the manners or events of the times. So two suitable pastimes for your Pancake Tuesday party are Mask-Making and Burlesqueing.

Divide your guests into teams of two or three couples to a team. Then explain that they are to be mummers and are to burlesque some contemporary persons, events, fads, or customs. But first they are each to make an appropriate mask to wear during their performances.

Provide each player with a paper bag large enough to fit over his head, and at hand have an ample supply of scissors, crayons, colored construction paper, and paste. Each player cuts holes in his paper bag for his eyes to see through, and then, with the crayons designs his mask, cutting out of the construction paper ears, noses, horns, or what he wishes, to paste on the mask.

Each team in turn now dons its masks and gives its performance while the other players try to guess what it is the team is burlesqueing.

After all the teams have performed, a vote is taken as to which team gave the best performance, and another vote is taken to determine who designed the best mask.

Valentine's Day

Valentine's Day is probably a Christian adaptation of the ancient Roman festival of the Lupercalia, which was celebrated annually on February 15 in honor of Lupercus, a rustic deity identified with the Greek god Pan. It was the custom on this occasion to put the names of young women in a box, from which men drew them as chance directed. For centuries this same custom was common in England and France, and became popular at many European courts. No one knows for sure how it happened that St. Valentine, an obscure martyr of the third century, was selected to supersede Lupercus, but it may be that *valentine* is a corruption of *galantin*, which means a lover (a gallant), and St. Valentine was chosen simply for his name to be the patron saint of sweethearts.

At one time the practice was, on St. Valentine's Day, for both sexes to make presents to each other; later only the man gave the present, and he was expected to remain faithful to the services of his Valentine for a whole year; and still later it became a general custom for both sexes to send to each other anonymous love notes and tokens.

Valentine's Day is sweethearts' day and also heralds the coming of spring. Therefore it is one of the best days of the year for celebrating and having a good time.

If you want to give a Valentine's party that will be out of the ordinary draw your ideas from the ancient origins of Valentine's Day and decorate your rooms with evergreens and flowers to suggest a woodland bower, and in a corner have Pan, with his pipes, sitting on a rock. This representation of Pan you, or one of your artistic friends, could paint on heavy cardboard and cut out. Cupid, with his bow and arrows, should be the center of attraction at the buffet table; and smaller cupids could be placed here and there among the room decorations.

When the guests arrive use Parted Couples (#34) to determine partners. Call the game Parted Valentines and have the names written on red, cut-out hearts. Place the male hearts in one box and the female hearts in another, and have the guests draw from these boxes as they arrive, the girls drawing from the females' box and the men drawing from the males' box. Have the guests wear their hearts on their sleeves and tell each to find his or her valentine.

When the parted couples have been united, have the Dressing Race (#13), only call it Elopement; and then play Hearty Words (#93).

Now provide everybody with colored construction paper, paper doilies, picture magazines, tubes of paste, scissors, and crayons; and allow fifteen or twenty minutes for each guest to construct a pretty or comic valentine for his or her partner. Have the prettiest and the most comical valentines selected by vote, and then give each of the valentines to the person for whom it was intended, as a souvenir of the party.

Hang in the center of the room a large red heart made from heavy paper, through a hole in the center of which thread half as many long lengths of twine or ribbon as there are guests, being careful not to tangle them. Each girl takes hold of the end of one of the lengths of twine or ribbon on one side of the heart and the men do the same on the other side of the heart. At a signal they all pull taut the pieces of string or ribbon, tearing the paper heart, so the lengths of twine or ribbon are freed, and each player can discover what girl or man is on the other end of his or her string. These now become partners for the game of Proposals (#57).

Complete your program of pastimes with Last Lines and then serve the refreshments buffet style.

Last Lines. Give each couple a pencil and paper. Explain that you will read all but the last lines of several familiar verses and that each couple is to write down what the last lines are and number their answers in the order in which the verses are read. You can select your own verses or quotations. The following are suggestions:

1. *Her voice is low and sweet—*
    And she's a' the world to me;
And for bonnie Annie Laurie

....

2. *Helen, thy beauty is to me*
    Like those Nicaean barks of yore,
That gently, o'er a perfumed sea,
    The weary, wayworn wanderer bore

....

3. *Drink to me only with thine eyes,*
      And I will pledge with mine;
    Or leave a kiss but in the cup

....

4. *No, the heart that has truly loved never forgets,*
      But as truly loves on to the close,
    As the sunflower turns to her god when he sets

....

5. *Gin a body meet a body*
      Comin' through the glen,
    Gin a body kiss a body,

....

6. *Of all the girls that are so smart*
      There's none like pretty Sally;
    She is the darling of my heart,

....

7. *The mind has a thousand eyes*
      And the heart but one;
    Yet the light of a whole life dies

....

8. *Then be not coy, but use your time,*
      And while ye may, go marry;
    For having lost but once your prime,

....

9. *Here's to the maiden of bashful fifteen,*
      Here's to the widow of fifty;
    Here's to the flaunting extravagant quean,

....

10. *None shall part us from each other;*
       One in love and life are we—
     All in all to one another,

....

The last lines are: (1) I'd lay me down and dee; (2) To his own native shore; (3) And I'll not look for wine; (4) The same look which she turned when he rose; (5) Need the world ken? (6) And she lives down in our alley; (7) When love is done; (8) You may forever tarry; (9) And here's to the housewife that's thrifty; (10) I to thee and thou to me.

Not more than two minutes should be allowed for writing down each last line. Each couple scores 5 points for every correct last line they write.

After the last lines have been read and the papers scored, you may then ask the couples to write opposite the last lines on their papers the authors of each last line, five points being scored for each correct answer.

The authors are: (1) William Douglas; (2) Edgar Allan Poe; (3) Ben Jonson; (4) Thomas Moore; (5) Robert Burns; (6) Henry Carey; (7) Francis William Bourdillon; (8) Robert Herrick; (9) Richard Brinsley Sheridan; (10) William Schwenck Gilbert.

May Day

All over the world, for centuries, the spring-tide has been celebrated in festive fashion and many of the customs now associated with our May Day have been derived from ancient traditions and practices. Among these customs are the choosing of the Queen of the May, the gathering of spring flowers, the erection of Maypoles, and dancing. Although May Day is not an official holiday in the United States, it is still celebrated with Maypole dancing, singing, pageantry, or theatrical performances in many places.

A May Day (or May-time) party should, of course, be an outdoor party—a picnic supper in the woods, by a stream, would be just right. If you have a May party in your house, decorate your rooms with plenty of spring flowers. It was an old May Day custom for individuals to fill small baskets with flowers, and then hang these May baskets on the doors of their friends' houses. You might ask each of the guests invited to your May party to bring a May basket, and, after exhibiting them, offer a prize to the owner of the basket judged to be the prettiest.

The most popular May Day pastimes have been dancing, hoop-rolling, archery, and theatrical performances. These suggest the amusements for your party. If your party is indoors, you will have to make substitutions for the hoop-rolling and archery. In their places have a Hoop Relay Race (#20) and Flower Darts (#18). Another appropriate game would be to exhibit a dozen or more different kinds of flowers (or pictures of them), each numbered, and see which guest is able, in a limited time, to write down the correct name of each flower.

Morris dances are the correct thing for the dancing, but the more popular American square dances will be more enjoyed. For the theatrics, charades are recommended, although a prearranged and rehearsed, original skit, employing local quips and good-natured personal gibes, would be more in keeping with tradition.

For supper, indoors, serve, buffet style, a gaily garnered chicken salad, Parker House rolls, orange jelly in molds, topped with whipped cream and a maraschino cherry, cup cakes iced with different colored icings, and coffee. During the dancing, later in the evening, serve a refreshing punch and cheese crackers.

Easter Day

Easter, the day of Christ's rising from the dead, is the queen of Christian festivals. It is the season of rebirth; a time when everyone should be joyful. Among the many interesting customs associated with this day are rising early in the morning to see the sun dance, which was the origin of the sunrise services that are now held in so many places; putting out the fires and decorating the hearths with flowers; "lifting" or "heaving"; kissing; playing handball; and the presentation of ornamented eggs, called Pasche Eggs.

The curious custom of heaving was practiced in this manner. Two men (or women), joining their hands across each others wrists, make the person to be heaved sit in this improvised chair, and then lift her (or him) up aloft three times. Then, setting the person down, each

43

man kisses her (or each girl kisses him) and demands a forfeit. Sometimes, instead of crossed hands, a real chair was used. The kiss is the appropriate Easter salutation in the Greek Church. On Easter everyone, as he met his friend, saluted him with a kiss on each side of his face, and repeated the words, "Christ is risen."

The Easter sport of handball seems to be the origin of the present games of cricket and baseball. It was not the same game of handball we know today. The ball was thrown from one to another. We are told that at Easter "bishops and deans took the ball into the Cathedral [Chester], and at the commencement of the antiphon, began to dance, throwing the ball to the choristers, who handed it to each other during the time of the dancing and antiphon"; and "the bishops and archbishops on the Continent used to recreate themselves in the game of handball with their inferior clergy."

A good time to celebrate Easter with a party would be right after the Easter morning church service. Invite your friends to come for brunch after the service.

Serve brunch on attractively decorated card tables, covered with green crepe paper crossed with yellow streamers. On each table place a small centerpiece of spring flowers surrounded by gaily colored hard-boiled eggs.

After brunch each guest takes one of the colored eggs from the center piece and all play Egg Cracking.

Egg Cracking. Each player has a hard-boiled egg. With this egg he must try to crack the egg of whatever other player challenges him. The challenger holds his egg in his hand, end up. The challenged then hits the challenger's egg with the end of his own egg. If the challenged cracks the egg of the challenger, he wins the challenger's cracked egg; but, if his own egg is cracked, he must turn it over to the challenger. The players continue to challenge one another until only one uncracked egg is left. Whoever possesses that egg is declared winner. Another way to play this game is to give each player two or three eggs to begin with, and see who can win the greatest number of cracked eggs, before losing the eggs he started with.

After playing Egg Cracking, play "Heaving in the Modern Manner" (#113).

Other games to play are Balloon Batting (#4), in place of handball; Egg Relay Race (#14); Getting the Most Out of EASTER DAY (see who can write down the greatest number of good English words of three or more letters each, spelled with the letters used in EASTER DAY); and Easter Bonnets.

Easter Bonnets. Have on a large table a supply of odds and ends of paper (including crepe paper), cloth, etc; and pins, tubes of paste, and enough scissors to go around. Allow each player 15 minutes in which to make an Easter bonnet. Then have the girls model the bonnets and give a prize for the best bonnet, for the best bonnet made by a girl, and for the best bonnet made by a man.

In olden days in England the regular prize for Easter games was the Tansy-cake, a sugar cake made of flour, butter, sugar, sherry, cream, and tansies. For your party have ready a basket filled with sugar cakes to be distributed as prizes.

Halloween

Everyone—well, nearly everyone—in one way or another celebrates Halloween, the time when, according to ancient superstition, witches, devils, fairies, and other imps of earth and air hold their annual convention and field day, and indulge in as many pranks, capers, discourtesies, quips, and practical jokes as are practiced by the fun-loving *voyageurs of La Société des Quarante Hommes et Huit Chevaux* at their annual turn out.

The celebration of Halloween can be traced back to the Roman festival in honor of Pomona, the goddess of fruit trees, and to the Druid's autumn festival in honor of the Sungod. It was the practice of the Druids on this occasion to light bonfires as an expression of their thankfulness for the harvest. They also believed that Samhain, the lord of death, at this time gathered together the souls of sinners who had died during the year and had been compelled to inhabit the bodies of lower animals. Halloween, we are told, is the night on which the spirits manifest themselves, and in divers ways communicate with mortals regarding what the future holds in store.

Halloween is just the evening for a Superstition Party. The tenor of a Superstition Party, like the spirit of Halloween, is mystery, sorcery, and supernaturalism. The more spooky, scary, and mysterious you can make the setting of your party, the more fun there will be.

Lights should be dim and well screened by shades representing pumpkin heads, the heads of black cats or witches, bats, etc. There should be plenty of lighted Jack-o-lanterns. Other things to incorporate in your decorations are broomsticks, cut-out skulls, a scarecrow or two, a couple of scary ghosts, made of pillows and sheets, hung in dimmed hallways, toy bats and spiders, hung from the ceilings of the rooms where you entertain, and cobwebs which are easily made with light string or heavy thread. Hanging lengths of black thread from doorways and ceilings will suggest spider-webs when unexpectedly touched by the face or hands. Instead of using a lot of paper streamers and such, decorate your rooms with autumn leaves, pumpkins, cabbages, apples, and large turnips.

A large Jack-o-lantern, standing on a bed of autumn leaves, ringed with red apples will be an attractive centerpiece for the supper table. Four tall, orange-colored candles, stuck in cored red apples, will make a good showing. Cut the bottoms of the apples, so the apples will stand steady. Small, colored, paper cups with cutout owls or witches or bats pasted on them should be filled with nuts and set at each place. A toy mouse at each place could have attached to it a place card. Favors could be toy snakes, toads, spiders, bats, wishbones, four-leaved clovers, and the like.

Invite your guests to come in costumes or not, as you wish. If you decide on costumes, suggest they come dressed as Halloween characters—witch, ghost, black cat, devil, scarecrow, fairy, goblin, skelton, etc.

To start the proceeding, and pick partners, play Meeting of Ghosts (#29). Then give each couple a piece of

46

string, about 3 feet long, at the center of which is tied a Life Saver (or other piece of candy). The man puts one end of the string in his mouth, and the girl puts the other end of the string in her mouth. At the signal to go, they each try to gather up the string with their lips until one reaches and bites the Life Saver. During this activity the hands must be held clasped behind the backs of each contestant. Of course, whoever first bites the Life Saver wins it.

Next play Candle Blowing (#108); Apple or Flour? (#106); Spear the Ring (#123); and Threading Pumpkin Seeds.

Threading Pumpkin Seeds. Give each man a threaded needle and to his partner a cup of wet pumpkin seeds. At the signal to start, each girl takes one seed from her cup and gives it to her partner, who takes it and spears it with his needle, running it down the thread. As soon as he has done this, the girl hands him another seed to thread. This continues until time is called. Each couple then counts the number of seeds it has threaded. Whichever couple has threaded the greatest number of seeds is declared winner. A seed dropped on the floor must be recovered by the distaff member of the couple which dropped it, before another seed may be threaded.

Now play *Superstitions.* Supply pencil and paper to each couple and see which couple can write down in ten minutes the greatest number of common superstitions, such as "see a pin and pick it up, all the day you'll have good luck"; to walk under a ladder brings bad luck; if you break a mirror you will have bad luck for seven years; 13 is an unlucky number; it is bad luck to open an umbrella indoors; you will have bad luck if you light three cigarettes from one match; a bride at her wedding must wear "something old and something new, something borrowed and something blue", otherwise the marriage will not be successful; etc.

How Do You Feel? will provide a spooky climax to your activity program. Play it in the following manner.

Announce to the assemblage in your best melodramatic manner that the hacked body of a man has just been found in your yard and the police have brought in parts of it with the hope that by means of them someone present can identify the unfortunate victim. Explain that you will pass around the piece in separate bags, and each person is to put his hand in each bag and feel what is there. No person is to look into any of the bags, and no person is to name or comment on what is in each bag.

Now bring in eleven bags, in each of which is one of the following: some chilled, cooked macaroni; two grapes which have been peeled; a large fig; a piece of a peeled, raw potato, cut in the shape of a big toe; six or eight spools strung together with wire or cord; a false mustache; a damp kid glove filled with sand; a dozen kernels of dried corn; the drumstick from a chicken; a small piece of shell; and the head of a small cauliflower.

After the last guest has felt the object in the last bag, hand each guest pencil and paper and instruct him to write down a list of all the objects he felt and what part of the body of the recently deceased he thought each object represented.

The macaroni represented the arteries; the grapes, the eyes; the fig, an ear; the potato, the big toe; the strung spools, the backbone; the mustache, the mustache; the glove, the hand; the corn, the teeth; the drumstick, a bone from the hand (or foot); the shell, a finger (or toe) nail; and the cauliflower, the brain.

Christmas Eve

Of all the seasons of the year, the Christmas season is the gayest, merriest, and the happiest. This, "the most venerable and tremendous of all festivals," is the festival of laughter, good cheer, good will, and hospitality. It is an old, old custom to keep open house at this time of year. We are told that a Sir William Hollis, who kept his house at Houghton Chapel, Nottinghamshire, "in great splendor and hospitality," began Christmas at Halloween and continued it until Candlemas Day, during which time any man was permitted to stay in the house

refreshments, which are served right in the kitchen, catch-as-catch-can, and eaten anywhere the guests wish to sit.

Showers may be held at any time and for almost any purpose. There might be—and has been many times—a Bridge Shower, held at luncheon time, when the guest of honor is invited for luncheon, and, when she arrives, finds herself in the midst of a shower of presents, such as bridge score-pads, cards, bridgetable covers, ashtrays, etc. Just remember that the success of a shower depends upon surprise, real friends, and informality.

A Sinners' Party

At one time and/or another every one has an urge to jump over the traces, as the old saying goes, and qualify as a champion sinner. Usually virtue steps in and very little comes of it all. By having a Sinner's Party, you can offer your friends a chance of at least appearing as the sinners they have at some time wanted, or pretended, to be.

In your invitation, ask each of your guests to come to the party dressed as his or her favorite sinner: Adam, Eve, Rasputin, Faust, Mr. Hyde, Louis XV, Salome, Al Capone, Scarlett O'Hara, Lucrezia Borgia, Don Juan, Robin Hood, Henry VII, Blue Beard, Lady Hamilton, Cleopatra, Desdemona, Captain Kidd, Hitler, Stalin, etc., etc.

This party offers wide scope for originality and humor in the decorations. The color scheme should be black and red. Three walls of the room may be decorated with red devils, imps, serpents, devils' tridents, etc. On the fourth wall there could be a cartoon in white on a black background of Saint Peter at the Pearly Gates, closed, of course, on which is hung a sign, saying *No Admittance*. On either side of this there could be stars and zodiac symbols.

The supper table is covered with flaming red crepe paper, crisscrossed with black streamers. The candles, of course, should be red. For the centerpiece fill a cauldron with red apples. The place cards are folded

53

white cards with a red devil cutout pointing at the name. On the card write *Sinner So-and-So*, instead of just the name: Sinner May Burtt, Sinner Toby Thomas, etc.

Meeting of Sinners. When the guests arrive pin on the back of each the name of a wellknown sinner, and follow the directions for Meeting of Ghosts (#29).

Then give each guest a list of things which have been placed inconspicuously about the living room (see House Treasure Hunt #22). These things could be a cork-tipped cigarette, a pair of red dice, a Jack of Spades, a hangman's noose (made of heavy thread or light string), a pair of toy handcuffs, a policeman's whistle (any whistle), a gat (toy revolver or cap pistol), a black face-mask, a false mustache, a blackjack, and a thumb print.

Now supper can be served. The guests find the following menu at each plate.

MENU

BEELZEBUB COCKTAIL [1]

DEVILED CRABMEAT IN SHELLS

GREEN MAGIC [2]　　　　BARS SINISTER [3]

FALLEN ANGEL CAKE [4]

WITCHES' BREW [5]

During supper, each guest is given a slip of paper on which he writes the names of the three persons who in his opinion wears the best make-up and costume. The three winners of this balloting are announced at the end of supper.

After supper the guests play Categories (#83), using the word MURDER and having for the categories: Notorious Sinners, Crimes and Misdeeds; Titles of Murder or Detective Novels, Reptiles, and Cities. Other words to use are FELON, THIEF, CRIME, etc.

They can play Decapitations (#89), and Who's Next? (#50), only call it, Who's a Sinner?; and Proverbial His-

---

[1] Highly seasoned chilled tomato juice. [2] Green salad with French dressing. [3] Cornsticks of corn muffin mix. [4] Angel cake with chocolate ice cream. [5] Coffee.

trionics. Divide the guests into two teams and give each team a different list of half a dozen proverbs, such as: Hell is paved with good intentions; A rolling stone gathers no moss; The pot calls the kettle black; There's many a slip 'twixt cup and lip; You can't have your cake and eat it too; Satan finds some evil for idle hands to do; etc. One or more members of the first team acts out one of the proverbs given to his team, and the second team tries to guess what the proverb is: Then the second team acts a proverb for the first team to guess.

Finish off the party (and maybe some of your guests) with Murder (#30).

Shipwreck Party

The perfect place and time for a shipwreck party is outdoors on a moonlight night, preferably on a beach, where cooking can be carried on over an open fire, and where the color scheme and decorations are attended to by nature.

Write the invitation in verse or prose on a ragged piece of crumpled wrapping-paper. It might be something like this:

> A number of the passengers and crew of the Good Ship Merrywinkle, foundered at night, are making for Pine Needle Beach [place of the party] in life boats commanded by Captain John Smith [the host] and First Mate Mary Smith [the hostess,] and expect to land at 6 P.M. on [date of the party], ill-clad but none the worse for wear. Ira and Myra Cumtoo [couple to whom invitation is sent] are expected to be one of the shipwrecked company.

When the guests arrive they are told to forage for food. They will find hidden in the sand (not too well hidden!) a crate, or maybe several small wooden boxes, in which will be found cans of corned beef hash, baked beans, and condensed milk; packages of hard-tack (pilot crackers), coffee, and sugar; a frying pan, coffee pot, and can-opener; bananas and coconuts in the shell; and whatever cups, plates, and eating utensils are to be needed—all presumably jettisoned from the foundered ship and washed ashore.

While the shipwrecked company forages for the supplies, the captain and first mate make ready the fire and get it going. When the supplies are brought in, the ship's chef and his assistants prepare the food over the open fire.

At the end of the meal, the first mate, by way of a surprise, brings forth from a special hiding place a fine banana-coconut pie for dessert, all ready for serving.

After the meal, games are in order, and any of the following will be enjoyed until it is time to put out the fire and go home.

Bucket Brigade. Form two teams and have them sit in a row opposite each other. Give the end player of each team a beach pail and shovel. At the signal to begin, each end player fills his pail with sand, using only the shovel for the purpose, and when the pail is full he passes it, by the handle, to the player next to him, who passes it to the next player. So the pail is passed from one player to the next, always by the handle, until it reaches the player at the head of the line, who dumps the sand out of the pail, gets up, runs to the end of the line, sits down, refills the pail with sand, and starts it up the line again. This continues until the first player to fill the pail gets his opportunity of dumping the sand out of the pail. The team whose "first man" does this first wins. If during the game a pail is dropped, or the sand is spilt out of it, the pail must be passed back, from player to player, to the end of the line for refilling.

Touch the Third (#44).

Shell Out. Have each player find a shell. Draw with a stick a straight line in the sand. Then each player in turn stands at the line with his feet together and his toes touching the line. He falls forward, catching and balancing himself by his left hand and arm only. Once his left hand touches the ground it must not be moved.

Now without losing his balance, he extends his right arm forward as far as he can and places his shell, which he has been holding in his right hand, on the sand. After the last player has placed his shell, all the shells are picked up excepting the shell farthest away from the line. Then each player is given another chance of placing his shell, in the manner described, out beyond this remaining shell. If any one succeeds, the owner of the remaining shell is given a chance to beat the new record. Whoever places his shell the farthest out beyond the line wins the game. A player who loses his balance, moves his left hand after it touches the ground, moves either foot away from the line, or touches the ground with any part of his body excepting his feet and left hand is disqualified.

Touring With the Alphabet (#77), Ghosts (#81), Storytelling (Tell a story and challenge any one to "top it"). No campfire group will be satisfied without a song. So end the party with a few old-time nautical ballads.

Circus Party

Circus parties are always fun, because they are colorful, permit the girls a wide choice of costumes becoming to them, give the men a chance to be as clever and funny as they can be, and offer the best opportunity for variety in entertainment. They can be elaborate outdoor affairs or relatively simple indoor parties.

For a relatively simple indoor circus party you might send out an invitation designed to represent an advertising "broadside" or "flyer." On a sheet of white foolscap paper (about 12″ by 15″) print with colored ink or crayon something like this—

ONE NIGHT ONLY

APRIL 10

AT THE JAMES SPIFF'S LOT

123 CLARKSIDE ROAD

BUNKUM & BLARNEY'S

GAITY CIRCUS

57

FEATURING
BEAUTIFUL GIRLS
WILD MEN
PLENTY OF CLOWNS
BARRELS OF FUN
WEARERS OF CIRCUS COSTUMES ADMITTED FREE
DOORS OPEN AT 8 P. M. SHARP

This invitation should be gaily decorated with painted drawings (or cutouts) of clowns, monkeys, pink elephants, balloons, etc.

The playroom or living room should represent the Main Tent. This can be achieved by removing all the furniture, and hanging from the center of the ceiling to the walls, at the height of the top of the windows, alternating red and white broad strips of crepe paper. Around the walls where the crepe paper strips end, festoon swags of narrow blue crepe paper streamers, by fastening them at regular intervals with gold pasteboard or paper stars. On the walls hang real or imitation circus posters, silhouettes of clowns, animals, etc., and clusters of varied colored balloons. The doorways may be hung with blue crepe paper streamers, and over each an appropriate sign can be hung: To The Sideshow, To The Animal Tent, etc.

Another room, where refreshments are to be served, may be decorated in a similar manner, excepting, by the walls, there should be set up several booths, or tables, decorated with crepe paper, flowers, and novelties. One of these booths should be for liquid refreshments; another for hot dogs, peanuts and popcorn; another for potato salad to be served on paper plates; and one more booth for ice cream and cup cakes.

A third room, if available, can be arranged to represent the sideshow tent. One end of this room should be reserved for dart throwing, an always popular sport. At the other end arrange a table for Comparisons (#85). On the floor, along one side of the room lay out the Horse Racing (#21) track.

Welcome your guests in the Main Tent, hang names on their backs and start them playing What's My Name? (#47). Then have a Tight Rope Race (#43). After that

58

they will want to sit down, so give them each a list of Jumbled Words (using words associated with a circus, such as LWCNO, *clown*; PALICOLE, *calliope*; TA-RIMNERGS, *ringmaster*; CARTBOA, *acrobat*; etc.

After fifteen minutes with Jumbled Words, have a Turtle Race (#45). Then take the crowd inside the sideshow tent and test their wits on Comparisons (#85). After that they can play darts and Horse Racing (#21) until it is time to partake of the refreshments in the refreshment tent.

After the refreshments the costumes may be judged and prizes for the evening awarded.

Inside Out, Upside Down Party

At this party, which is suitable for April Fool's Day, everything possible is done the wrong way around. Costumes are worn inside out, wrong side front, or even upside down. The guests are received at the back door, instead of at the front door.

The invitation is written backward and upside down.

WILL YOU COME TO AN
INSIDE-OUT, UPSIDE-DOWN
BACKSIDE-TO PARTY,
AT THE POST'S HOUSE
SANDSTORM AVENUE
SATURDAY EVENING
APRIL FIRST
AT SEVEN O'CLOCK
DRESSED IN THE
MANNER OF THE WORD
BRING WITH YOU, WRAPPED AS A GIFT
A WHITE ELEPHANT
SOMETHING YOU DON'T WANT
AND HAVE NO USE FOR
PLEASE REPLY

The color scheme for the decorations is black and white. White table covering; black paper napkins; black place cards with white dunce caps, upside down, and names written backwards in white ink; and a paper jack-horner-pie centerpiece in the form of an upside-down dunce cap balanced in a bowl full of nuts with black ribbon streamers leading to the various place cards at the table. In the dunce cap are whistles, puzzles, and trick gadgets. The table is set as if to accommodate left handed persons: forks on the right, tumblers on the left, etc.

The first activity of this party is Associated Words (#2), the word on each card written backwards: DAERB, RETTUB, EVIG, EKAT, etc. On the reverse side of each card write the name of the guest who is to wear the card, and make sure that each guest gets his right card, so that the choice of partners will correspond with your arrangement of place cards at the supper table.

After the partners have found each other, all go in for supper.

The fun of this supper is in the serving. After the guests are seated, covered soup bowls are set before them. When the covers are lifted the bowls are found to contain hot coffee! Next "dessert" is served—large cream puffs, with a hidden filling of chicken salad! When the surprise is over, hot green peas and additional salad are passed, with rolls or melba toast. After this course, the "first" course is served—fruit cup with sherbet. And more coffee, of course.

After supper the following games are played:

Opposites (#73).

Upside-down Alphabet. Sitting as they were for the first game, the players are asked to recite the alphabet backwards. The last player on team A, says Z, then the last player on team B must instantly say Y, and the next to the last player on team A says X, and the next to the last player on team B says W, and so on. There must be no hesitation in calling the letters. A player who hesitates or calls the wrong letter is immediately eliminated. When the alphabet has been completed, the players are asked to repeat the alphabet backwards, but this time omitting every other letter. Then they are asked again to repeat it backwards, leaving out all the vowels. And, finally, they are asked to repeat it backwards, leaving out all the consonants. If any players survive so far, ask them to repeat the alphabet backwards once more, but this time omitting all the letters the capitals of which are commonly written in print with one or more horizontal lines (Z, T, L, I, H, F, E, A).

Alphabet Cards (#1). The guests, having become thoroughly familiar with the alphabet in reverse, are required in this game to spell all the words given backwards.

Drawing the Invisible (#91). The artist is required to draw the object upside down, and his partner must give him directions accordingly.

Tightrope Racing (#43). The guests are first asked to try this backward (walk backwards along the line while looking through the large lenses of a pair of opera glasses) and then do it forward.

To select the most original costume, have each guest stand up and let the others express their opinions by applauding. The wearer of the costume which receives the loudest applause is declared winner.

Lunatic's Exchange (#25) is just the event to round off this tomfoolery and send your guests home still laughing.

A Superlative Party

It is human to want to excel at something, so a superlative party should provide a superlatively enjoyable evening for anyone who attends.

Your invitation will invite your guests to come in a superlative manner, made up and costumed to represent the fatest, the tallest, the most comical, the most beautiful, the most elaborately dressed, the poorest, the toughest, the most villainous, the most snobbish, the most bejeweled, the sportiest, the timidest, the most ghostly, the most angelic, or the most anything else each can think of.

Decorations for this party should be exaggerated to

the point of burlesque. Gaudy crepe paper streamers; an enormous centerpiece, or jack-horner pie with superlatively absurd favors in it.

Meeting of Ghosts (#29) will start the party off right and also determine partners. Other games for this extravagant affair are Confabulation (#65), Guessing the Leader (#19), Proposals (#57), Who Am I? (#80), and Clothing (#84). After playing these games have your guests vote on the most successful make-up and costume, and then serve supper.

As-You-Were Party

Where Daylight Saving is practiced there is no better excuse for a gay celebration than the occasion of turning back the clocks an hour on the last night of the Daylight season. Turning back the clocks at midnight adds, of course, an additional hour to the celebrating period.

The theme of an As-You-Were party is turning time backward, so this is an especially appropriate party for the last night of the Daylight season. For this party invite your guests to turn back the calendar and come to the festivities disguised as well as possible to look the way they did ten, fifteen, or twenty years ago. If your guests are in their twenties, have them come as they were when they were ten to twelve years of age. If they are in their thirties, have them come as they were when they were in their early teens. And if they are in their forties, have them come as they were when they were in their courtship days.

Ask each guest to bring with him a childhood photograph taken before he was ten years old. Collect the photographs as the guests arrive, keep them in two groups, the photographs of the girls in one, and the photographs of the men in the other.

After all of the guests have arrived, let each man draw, sight unseen, a photograph of a girl. Each man then tries to identify the subject of the photograph, who is to be his partner. Later in the evening, at an appropriate time, change partners by having the girls identify the men's photographs.

For entertainment after dinner, or before late refreshments, give your guests a list of twenty questions, pertaining to wellknown persons and events of the era, and see who can answer correctly the greatest number. Then play Balloon Batting (#4), Turtle Racing (#45), and Streamer Cutting (#41), and end up with Charades based on events (the more personal, the better) which happened in the as-you-were days.

Advertising Party

An advertising party offers rich possibilities for original costumes, amusing decorations, and interesting entertainment—all at no great expense.

Invite your guests to come in costumes representing the various professions and trades mentioned in newspaper want advertisements: doctors, artists, airline pilots, mechanics, waiters, bricklayers, trained nurses, models, airline hostesses, dancers, cooks, parlor maids, etc. Suggest what each guest might represent by clipping a want adv. from a newspaper and pasting it on to your invitations.

Or you may ask your guests to costume themselves to represent the name of any nationally advertised product, such as Gold Dust, Fairy Soap, Rinso Blue, Spic and Span, Victor Records, Black and White Scotch Whiskey, etc.; or they may represent characters featured in advertisements, such as the Gold Dust twins; Kleenex's Little Lulu; a Sunshine baker; the National Lead Company's Dutch boy; the *Philadelphia Bulletin*'s thin man who doesn't read the *Bulletin*; the Green Giant; the Planter's Peanut man; the Dutch Cleanser, who chases dirt; etc.

Your invitations could be typewritten in the form of "Personal" advertisements; something like this:

PERSONAL

There'll be a hot time in the old town if the beautiful blue-eyed blonde and her talented consort, who live at 49 Pupkin Parkway, come to 222 Tootle Lane at 7 o'clock in the evening of March 6, disguised as any fictitious characters made famous in national advertising.

The Gold Dust twins; the Planter's Peanut man; the Cliquot Eskimo; one of the Piel brothers, Harry or Bert; the Alkaseltzer boy who knows what's good for acid indigestion; Little Lulu; Carling's Red Cap Ale jockey; the Dutch Cleanser, who chases dirt; etc.)

The room decorations for an advertising party should feature mock advertising posters, which good-naturedly make sport of your guests. These posters can be made with cutouts and crayons, on sheets of heavy paper or Bristol board, and hung on the walls. The obsessed shutter-clicker would be advertised as the master of distortion photography; the speed-demon as the champion kiddy-car racer; the glamor girl as the beautician par excellence, who knows her paints and powders, etc.

Place favors may be miniature packages of standard products, which can be obtained from toy stores and novelty shops. The table centerpiece can be made up of bottled, canned, and packaged products taken from your own kitchen shelves, stacked in a low pyramid and surrounded by fruit and fruit leaves at the base of the pyramid.

The obvious game to play at an advertising party is Slogan Guessing (#100).

Then play Going to Market. Have hidden not wholly out of view, as many can labels, box-tops, and bottle-tops, from food and beverage products, as you can collect. Instruct the guests to hunt for these, and see who can find the greatest number and variety.

Follow this game with Building Pictures (#82), but call it *Advertising*; and instruct each guest (or each team) to design an illustrated advertisement, filling in the heading, slogan, and sale's talk, etc., with crayon.

Then play Essentially Different (#67), for, after all, isn't every product advertised as being essentially different from any other product in its own field?

And now will be a most appropriate time to play Proverbial Histrionics (#58), only call it *Sale's Appeal*; and, instead of dramatizing proverbs, have the players act out advertising slogans.

If there is time for another game, try *Absolutely Free.*

Give each guest pencil and paper and tell him to write, in a column, the letters in the words *absolutely free*. At the signal to start, each guest writes opposite each letter on his paper as many trade names of products as he can think of, which begin with the letter opposite which they are to be written. For example, opposite the letter A, a guest might write Alkaseltzer, Anacin, etc.; opposite B, he might write Bon Ami, Bendix, Band-Aid, etc.; and opposite S he might write Stopette, Schaefer, Socony, etc. The players must begin with the first letter, and, at the end of one minute, must move on to the second letter, and at the end of the second minute work on the third letter, and so on. The leader calls the time. The object of the game is to see who can recall the greatest number of trade names which begin with each of the letters given.

As a final activity the best costume should be selected by vote.

The menu for an advertising party should be made up entirely of trade-marked foods.

Twenty-First Birthday Party

There are certain milestones in the life of man that have such a special significance that they deserve special attention, which means a celebration, or a party—entering the "teens," graduating from school, coming of age, becoming engaged, etc.

The twenty-first birthday is one of those milestones. Twenty-one is a grand old age. It is the last milestone between youth and maturity. Before twenty-one, you are an infant, a child, an adolescent, or a youth. After twenty-one, you are a man or a woman, until you pass forty, when you will be middle-aged, early or late, until you become senile.

The twenty-first birthday should rate a party; and a really sophisticated, grown-up, good-fun party it ought to be. So forget all about customary, coming-of-age business, and ask your dearest friends to come to your house, in evening dress, about seven-thirty or eight o'clock in the evening of your birthday, for a bit of rug-cutting and other sports. You won't have to tell them it is your birthday. You want a celebration; not a reminder that you have lost your youth, which you haven't done, excepting for the calendar.

Then plan your party along these lines.

First decorate your living room, and as many other rooms as you will have need for, to represent the famous New York "21" Club. This will be very easy, because the "21" Club does not go in much for decorations. It is primarily a room with enough floor-space for dancing surrounded by tables at which luncheon, tea, dinner, or supper can be enjoyed between dances, or while watching the dancers.

Set up, and set, bridge-tables and chairs around the sides of the room, leaving the center free for dancing to phonographic music. A small vase holding two or three carnations, roses, or other flowers serves as a centerpiece for each table, and each table should have one candle on it. Leaning against the candlestick should be a piece of Bristol board, lettered, *Reserved*. Underneath the word Reserved should be written the names of the girls (only) who are to occupy the table. Noise-makers—horns, rattles, etc.—will serve for place favors, and each should be marked "21".

On the outside of the front door should be attached the numerals "21."

The lighting of the rooms should be dim. Exchange the regular light bulbs for blue, red, and amber bulbs.

When the guests arrive they are welcomed by your husband or boy friend, dressed in an imposing "doorman" uniform (rented), who sends them to the cloakroom, where a girl friend, impersonating a "hat-check girl," takes care of the coats and hats and cloaks and wraps, and directs the ladies to the "powder-room."

You receive the guests at the entrance to the living room and hang over the neck of each a card bearing a number.

The purpose of these cards is to choose partners. This is how it works. If there are to be twenty guests, prepare beforehand 10 cards of one color, say blue, each numbered from 1-10, inclusive; then prepare 10 cards of another color, say white, numbered from 11-20, inclusive. Give one of the blue cards to each male guest and one of the white cards to each female guest. Then the object is for each guest to find a card on which is a number, which, when added to the number on his or her card, will make 21. Whoever wears that card is to be his or her partner. For instance, Buzz Bonester is given a blue card with the number 5 on it. He hunts around until he finds a white card with the number 16 on it. The bearer of that white card, who will be a girl, of course, is his partner, and he escorts her to the table where her name appears on the *Reserved* sign.

When all the guests have arrived the phonograph is turned on for dancing.

After the first dance, everyone returns to the tables and each table group composes a congratulatory telegram, using the letters of your name, in the order in which they appear in your name, as the first letters of each word of the telegram.

The telegrams are then read, and the phonograph is turned on again for more dancing.

While the guests are dancing the cocktails are brought in and are put at each place. When the music stops, all return to the tables and enjoy the cocktails.

The phonograph starts again, and while the guests are dancing, the cocktail glasses are removed, and jellied consommé is placed on the tables.

When the music ends, the dancers return to their tables and partake of the consommé.

Then there is more dancing, while the consommé plates are removed and seafood and peas are placed on the tables.

The dancing stops and the seafood course is enjoyed.

During the next dancing period, the seafood plates are removed and the ice cream molds are placed on the tables. When every one has returned to his or her table, the birthday cake, brightly lighted with 21 candles, is brought in, and placed on the table of the honored guest, who cuts it.

Then there is more dancing while the tables are cleared and coffee cups, sugar, and cream are placed on the tables. When the dancing stops, the coffee is served.

When dancing is resumed, the tables are cleared, and a large tray with glasses and a big pitcher of ice water, or other beverage, is placed on an extra side table, for those who want to help themselves.

From here on dancing and conversation are the order of the evening, or what's left of it, which will not be very much.

If you can persuade a few gifted friends to perform stunts in between the courses, so much the better. It will carry out better the atmosphere of the night club—but maybe your guests would prefer to dance.

Wedding Anniversary Parties

There is no better reason for a celebration than a wedding anniversary, especially in these days when to remain married for any considerable period of time is the exception rather than the rule and worthy of very special commendation. According to ancient tradition each wedding anniversary has a particular significance. The first is the paper wedding; the second is the cotton wedding; the third, leather; the fourth, books; the fifth, wood; the tenth, tin; the fifteenth, crystal; the twentieth, china; the twenty-fifth, silver; the fiftieth, gold; and the sixtieth, diamonds. These designations indicate the theme and decorations for a party for each occasion, as well as the kind of gifts, favors, and prizes that are expected.

Obviously, a party for a paper wedding will be a livelier and less formal affair than a party to celebrate a Golden Wedding. An evening of stunts, and dancing would be a good way to celebrate a first wedding anniversary. A formal tea is a better way of celebrating the fiftieth anniversary.

A Paper Wedding Party

For your first wedding anniversary you will want to have present to help you celebrate as many of the original bridal party as are available—the matron of honor, the best man, the bridesmaids, and the ushers—as well as other close friends.

Because this is a paper wedding party, it might be a good idea to make it an oriental party, in costume or not, as you like. Decorate your rooms, attractively with paper streamers, festoons, and paper lanterns. Set the buffet supper table with paper doilies, paper napkins, and so on. A pretty centerpiece of paper flowers arranged in the form of a bridal bouquet would be appropriate.

When the guests arrive serve them cocktails and hors d'oeuvres, and, while they are enjoying these, play Cinderella's Slippers (#11) to pick partners for supper.

Then serve the buffet supper.

Consommé
Chicken Chow Mein
Pineapple
Wedding Cake

After supper the following games will be both appropriate and enjoyable. Consequences (#87), Picture Biographies (#97), Photographer (#35), the real bride and groom to pose first, Shadow Play (#59). Instead of dividing the guests into two teams, have each couple in turn go behind the sheet and represent, by tableau or silent action, a famous couple. The others try to guess the names of the famous couple represented.

Some famous couples to represent are, Major Hoople and Martha, Adam and Eve, Mr. and Mrs., Jiggs and Maggie, Dagwood and Blondie, Romeo and Juliet, Cyrano and Roxane, Samson and Delilah, Jack and Jill, Jack Sprat and his wife, and Punch and Judy.

A Silver Wedding Party

It is customary for a couple who have arrived at the twenty-fifth anniversary of their wedding to hold a reception, or high tea, to which they invite, among other intimates, as many of the persons who witnessed their wedding as are living and able to attend.

As far as possible the arrangements and plans should follow those of the wedding reception. The buffet table should be set in the manner of the buffet table at the first reception. The refreshments should also be the same. The bridal cake, as nearly like the original bridal cake as possible, should be the center of attraction.

The bride and groom, with as many of the original attendants as are present, stand on line as they did twenty-five years previously, and receive the guests.

After all the guests have been received, the bride, with the help of the groom, as once she did before, cuts the wedding cake. Often the couple on this occasion, before cutting the cake, renew their marriage vows.

A Golden Wedding Party

A golden wedding reception follows in general the pattern of a silver wedding reception, only it is likely to be more of a family affair. It is an occasion when the clan should gather to pay their respects and offer their congratulations—the children, the nephews and nieces, the young cousins, the grandchildren, and so on.

3. Active Games

1. Alphabet Cards

A SURE-FIRE, laugh generator is this spelling game. Divide the guests into two teams and provide each player with a card on which is painted or drawn a letter of the alphabet. These cards should be about 8½″ x 11″, with letters about 7″ tall, and should be strung so that they can be hung from the necks of the players. The cards should be so distributed as to provide both teams with exactly the same assortment of letters.

The teams line up, facing each other, with plenty of space between the two teams. The leader then calls out to Team A a word. The members of that team who hold the letters required to spell the word called immediately step forward and arrange themselves side by side so that their several cards, reading from left to right, will spell the word correctly. If the members of Team A succeed in doing this correctly in a period of one minute, they score one point for their team, and are given another word to spell. If they fail to spell a word correctly or consume more than one minute in arranging themselves, then Team B is given the next word to spell. And so it continues for the duration of the game, which should not be more than 30 or 40 minutes.

When selecting the letters choose from the ones most frequently used in writing: A, E, I, O, for the vowels; and C, D, H, L, M, N, R, S, T, B, for the consonants.

Of course, no word may be given for spelling which contains any letter which is not in the possession of one of the players. Therefore, to prevent embarrassment, as well as to save time, it is best to make up in advance a list of 30 or 40 words to be used, checking the spellings against the dictionary spellings, and arranging the words in order of difficulty, so that the game will begin with the easier words and proceed to the more difficult ones.

71

For a special occasion, such as a Washington's Birthday party, the letters supplied to the teams could be those which spell a word appropriate to the occasion. For instance, if you were giving a Washington's Birthday party for 16 persons, you would divide your guests into two teams of 8 players each; and to each team you would give the letters A, C, E, H, H, S, T, T (note that two persons on each team would have the letter H and two would have the letter T, which is permissible and will add to the fun). To demonstrate how the game is played, you would line up the two teams, so that their letters will be in alphabetical order, as given above. The first man on each team would hold A, the second C, the third E, and so on. Now you would ask each team to rearrange themselves so that each team spells the word HATCHETS. From then on you would play the game as described in the previous paragraphs.

When two players hold the same letter and only one of that particular letter is needed to spell a word called for, then the first holder of the letter to step into the correct position remains there to help spell the word and the holder of the duplicate letter must step out of the way. (Over 45 common English words of three or more letters can be spelled with the letters contained in the word HATCHETS.)

2. Associated Words

One of the entertaining ways by which to introduce partners to each other is to use cards with associated words written on them. Each guest upon his arrival is given, to hang around his neck, a card with one word on it. He must then look around for a person who carries a card upon which is written another word that is commonly associated with the word on his own card. For example, Tom Jones arrives and is given a card on which is the word BREAD. He hangs this around his neck and searches for a person with a card on which is another word commonly associated with the word BREAD, and soon discovers some one with a card with the word BUTTER. So BREAD and BUTTER are partners for the occasion; and, if they are not already known to each other, they might just as well introduce themselves and disclose their real names.

Pen and Ink	Black and White	Cream and Sugar
Hat and Coat	Pepper and Salt	Cigars and Cigarettes
Milk and Honey	Peanuts and Popcorn	Fish and Chips
Horse and Buggy	Ham and Eggs	Boots and Saddles
Give and Take	Thunder and Lightning	Ways and Means
Hustle and Bustle	Bigger and Better	Fine and Dandy
Rod and Gun	Free and Easy	Heaven and Earth
Hand and Foot	Ball and Chain	High and Dry
Life and Death	Thick and Thin	Up and Down

3. Ball Games

Rubber balls of different sizes are employed in a great variety of pastimes. Using whatever ordinary household equipment you have at hand, you can invent many diverting games. Here are a few ideas.

1. Place a table against a wall and on the end nearest the wall place a stocking box. The contestants, each in turn, stand a couple of feet away from the other end of the table and try to bounce a Jacks ball on the table in front of the stocking box in such a way as to make it land, and remain, in one of the compartments of the stocking box. Give each contestant three balls, and score five points for each ball that stays in the stocking box.

2. Place a scrapbasket on the floor, and, two or three feet in front of it, place a kitchen chair, with its back away from the scrapbasket. Each contestant in turn stands about eight feet away from the back of the chair and tries to bounce a tennis ball on the floor, between himself and the chair, so it will go over the chair and land in the scrapbasket. If the ball bounces out of the scrapbasket the contestant scores only five points, but if it remains in the basket he scores ten points. Each contestant is allowed five tries, and scores for every time

he succeeds in getting the ball into the basket, whether it stays in the basket or not.

3. Fasten a line of white tape across the floor, about eight feet from the wall and parallel to the wall. As many contestants as the width of the room will permit line up in back of this line. Each is given a tennis ball. The object of the game is to roll the ball against the baseboard of the opposite wall so that it will return to the tape line. The contestant whose ball stops rolling closest to the tape is declared the winner.

4. Stand in a row on the floor four paper bags (4" by 8"), seven inches apart and each two feet from the wall. The player stands seven or eight feet in front of the bags and bowls a tennis ball between any two of the bags so that the ball will bounce back from the wall and knock over one or more of the bags. If a bag is knocked over by a ball on its way to the wall the player does not score; he only scores on the bags knocked over by the ball on the rebound after the ball has passed between two bags. The two inside bags count five points each, and the outside bags ten points. Each player rolls the ball five times. The player who gets the highest total score wins.

4. Balloon Batting

This game may sound a bit silly, but don't forget that some of the silliest sounding games turn out to be the most fun. This game will appeal especially to the younger set.

Divide the players into two teams and line up the teams facing each other about 8 feet apart. Number the players of each team. Then instruct the even number players to exchange places; No. 2 of Team A changes places with No. 2 of Team B, No. 4 of Team A with No. 4 of Team B, etc.

To No. 1 of Team A give a red balloon and to No. 1 of Team B give a blue balloon. At a signal the game begins by the No. 1 players batting their balloons across to their No. 2 team-mates. The No. 2 players bat the balloons to their No. 3 team-mates, and so on to the end of the lines, when the balloons are batted back in reverse order. The team which first gets its balloon back to its No. 1 player wins.

After the game starts the balloons must be kept in motion in the air. If a balloon falls to the floor, it must be returned to the No. 1 player of the team to which it belongs and restarted down the lines. No one may touch a balloon out of turn or touch the balloon belonging to the opposing team.

5. Bamboo Tandem Race

Racing is real sport, any way you look at it. Who hasn't been thrilled by the sight of the horses galloping down the home stretch, or the sprinter breaking the tape at the end of a 100-yd. dash? Well, here is a sporty kind of a race that should provide plenty of thrills, and maybe more than one spill. It is for the stout of heart, so sedentary bridge players beware!

Divide your guests into teams of four or five persons each. Have the members of each team straddle an eight- or ten-foot bamboo pole; line up the teams; and, at a signal, start them galloping over a prescribed course, either across the room and back, if there is a room large enough, or around a triangular course, if you are entertaining outdoors.

The first team to reach home still intact wins the laurels. To the teams that don't finish give liniment, salve, and bandages, they'll probably need them.

6. Blind Man's Buff

You may be absolutely sure that this variation of that old-time sport, Blind Man's Buff, which was so dear to the hearts of your great-grandparents, will break down the formality of even a prig.

All the players but one, who is It, sit on chairs arranged in a circle, facing inwards. It stands in the center of the circle and is blindfolded. While he is being spun around several times to destroy his sense of direction, the players change places with each other to make matters more difficult for It. After the players have changed their places, they remain seated, and It, with his arms folded across his chest, fumbles about until he reaches one of the seated players, when he seats himself on the lap of that player. Now, without using his hands in any way, it is up to him to identify the player upon whose lap he is sitting. If he succeeds, that player becomes It, otherwise he must try again.

7. Bottling Clothespins

A collection of empty milk bottles and a bag of clothespins are needed for this entertaining game of skill. Divide your guests into teams of four players each. Have the first two teams stand in line facing each other, with ample space between the rows and between the players of each team, so the players will not interfere with each other. Each player stands with his feet together. A couple of inches in front of his toes is stood a milk bottle, and to him are given three clothespins. At a signal to begin, each player tries to drop his clothespins, one at a time, into his milk bottle from the height of his nose. He must keep his feet together and hold his body erect, but may bend his head forward. The clothespins are dropped head down. The team which succeeds in bottling the greatest number of its clothespins wins. A clothespin which fails to enter a bottle may not be played again.

8. Boy on a String

An exciting way of choosing partners by chance is to employ the tangled string method. Provide yourself with as many long lengths of string, of varied colors if possible, as you are to have couples at your party. Then, starting in one room run each of these strings around the furniture, winding it around the back of a chair, under and over a sofa, around the leg of a table, etc., and carry it through to another room, upstairs or on the same floor, continuing to attach it to various pieces of furniture and fixtures in the second room. The several strings should cross each other and should be attached to many objects, but care must be taken not to tie any knots or so entangle the strings as to make them difficult to disengage.

When the guests arrive the girls are assembled in the first room and the men are assembled in the second room. Each of the guests is then told to take an end of a string and, without breaking it, wind up the string, following it to wherever it leads. If the strings have been interestingly and cleverly placed, looped and crossed, the partners will not be revealed until they have met at a midway point. The first couple to disentangle and wind up their string deserves a prize.

9. Butter Fingers

This is probably the whackiest indoor adaptation of the ancient Potato Race ever thought up, and if, after indulging in it, your guests show no symptoms of mental deterioration they probably did not have any mentality to deteriorate when they started; and that would explain why they ever let you get them mixed up in the business.

Here is what happens. At one end of the room line up as many contestants as the room will accommodate, and at the other end of the room place side-by-side on the bare floor, directly in line with each contestant, five pasteboard, milk-bottle tops. Now give each contestant a pair of cotton or canvas working gloves, which should not fit too well.

Each contestant puts on his gloves, and, at the signal to start, dashes across the room, picks up one of the bottle-tops, rushes back to the starting line (where closed cardboard boxes, each with a small slot in its cover, have been placed), drops the bottle-top through the slot in his box, and goes back for the second bottle-top, and so on.

The first contestant to deposit successfully in his box all five of his bottle-tops, is declared winner, and deserves to keep his gloves as a reward.

This game can be played with teams, as a relay race. In that case as many bottle-tops are placed on the floor as there are members of each team. The first player only of each team is furnished gloves. When he retrieves his first bottle-top and has deposited it in his team's box, he takes off the gloves and hands them to the second player on his team, who must put them on and retrieve the second bottle-top. The winning team is the first to retrieve and box all of its bottle-tops.

10. Cat and Dog

The ideal place for playing this game is around the dining-room table. Two persons, one representing the dog and the other the cat, are blindfolded and stationed on opposite sides of the dining-room table, facing each other, with both hands touching the table. Having been blindfolded before stationed, neither one knows for sure where the other one is, or n which direction he is going to travel. They are told that, at a signal, the dog must try to catch the cat and the cat must try to keep away from the dog, but that each must have one hand touching the table at all times. At the signal to begin, the dog stealthily goes after the cat, and the cat, listening intently, tries to detect the approach of the dog and moves furtively to avoid him. During the proceedings, the spectators must endeavor to keep as quiet as they possibly can, which will require considerable self-control in view of the comic antics, contortions, and grimaces the cat and the dog will surely indulge in. If the dog is unable to touch the cat within a period of two and a half minutes, the cat wins; otherwise the dog is the victor.

11. Cinderella's Slippers

One of the most annoying (to females) weaknesses of the stronger sex is its unconcern regarding the details of feminine attire. How many are the lovely romances that have disintegrated because the boy friend repeatedly failed to notice the girl friend's new snood, kerchief, frill, furbelow, or party slippers! Capitalizing on this weakness of the male, you can have a considerable amount of sly fun at a party by introducing this interesting activity.

Seat all of your lovely lady guests in a row of chairs, side-by-side, and have their elegant gentlemen friends stand behind the chairs with their backs towards their respective partners. Now instruct the ladies to remove their shoes, which you collect and, mixing them, place in a heap about 10 feet or so in front of the seated ladies. The gentlemen are told to be discreet, as gentlemen should be, and under no circumstances peek over their shoulders to see what is going on.

After the shoes have been well mixed, the gentlemen are instructed to race to the heap of footwear and find the shoes which belong to their respective partners.

Here the fun begins. Each gentleman will think he has a pretty good idea of what his partner's shoes resemble and there will be a wild scramble, and, no doubt, an argument or two, at the footwear pile; and then surprise and confusion when the selected slippers are found not to fit. When this happens, the chooser of the shoes must find the feet to which they belong, and when he has done this, the owner of those feet then becomes his new partner.

The first gentlemen to shoe his partner with her own shoes deserves a very special reward.

This is an excellent game to play when it is desired to mix up the couples and change partners.

12. Community Treasure Hunt

Treasure hunting has engaged the interest and spurred the imagination of man since the beginning of time and has been the cause of high adventure and excitement, as well as of much mischief. Many forms of treasure hunting, free from the element of mischief, are admirably suited for party use. This one has proved to be one of the most popular forms.

Make up a list of 20 or 25 not too frequently seen articles, and have as many copies made of this list as you will need to supply your guests. The articles chosen should be such as are likely to be found in your community, but, because of their oddity, scarcity, or age, are not likely to be found too easily: the lacings for a corset, for instance; or a World War I silver discharge lapel button; or a hair from the head of a redheaded girl; or a collapsible opera hat; or a last-year's wall calendar.

Divide your guests into teams of two, three, or four members, depending on the total number of participants, and give to each team a copy of the list of articles to be found. At a given signal, the teams sally forth and search the community for the treasures. A time limit of two hours is set and all are instructed to report back before the expiration of that time. The first team to return with all the treasures on the list, or with the greatest number of the treasures, wins.

Before they start hunting, the members of each team decide among themselves which articles each will look for, and then separate and hunt individually.

In making up the list of treasures care must be taken to be specific in the descriptions, so that there will be no misunderstanding among the hunters as to the articles which they are to seek.

Suggested Articles for a Treasure Hunt

Something solid no one in the whole wide world has ever seen before and which, after it has been shown, no one in the whole wide world will ever see again. (Shell a nut, show the kernel, and immediately eat the kernel.)
A picture of a house in which Thomas Jefferson lived. (There is a picture of Monticello on an issue of United States five-cent pieces.)
A man's watch chain.
An ice pick.
A photograph of a friend taken before the age of three.
A pair of ladies silk stockings.
A piece of coal.
A top hat.
A parakeet's feather.
A woman's fan.

A last-year's automobile license plate.
A sand flea in a bottle (or some other small animal).
A baby's bottle nipple.
A man's cane.
A leaf from a red maple tree.

13. Dressing Race

If these high-jinks don't convulse your guests with laughter, nothing will.

Divide your guests into two teams of an equal number of couples. Line the teams up at one end of the room and place two chairs at the other end of the room.

Give the first couple of each team a traveling bag, in which is packed two night caps, two extra large nightgowns, two pairs of oversize slippers, and two dressing gowns.

At the signal to start, the two couples carry their bags to the chairs at the opposite end of the room, open the bags, take off their shoes, dress themselves in the nightgowns, nightcaps, slippers, and dressing gowns, run once around their chairs, remove the dressing gowns, slippers, nightgowns, and nightcaps, put on their own shoes, repack the traveling bags, and rush back to their teams, where they surrender the traveling bags to the next couples, who must repeat their performance.

This continues until the last couple of one team returns to the starting line with their repacked bag. The team to which that couple belongs is of course the winner.

Let there be no nonsense among the players—the clothes must be put on properly; and if a nightgown is found to be inside out when unpacked it must be turned right-side-out before it can be donned.

14. Egg Relay Race

Hard (15 minutes) boiled eggs are a must for this devil-may-care challenge to disaster.

Form teams and have half of each team stand at one end of the room and the other half directly opposite at the other end of the room. To every player give a tea-spoon, and then to the leader of each team give instructions to hold his teaspoon by its handle between his teeth. Also instruct him to keep his hands clasped behind his back. Now place a hard-boiled egg in the bowl of each leader's spoon; and tell each leader that, at the signal to go, he is to race across the room, keeping his hands clasped behind his back, without dropping his egg. When each leader reaches the opposite end of the room, he unclasps his hands, removes the egg from his spoon, and places it in the bowl of the teaspoon of his teammate who must then be holding his, or her, teaspoon between his, or her, teeth, and his, or her, hands must be clasped behind his, or her, back.

The teammate rushes back across the room, balancing the egg in his, or her, teaspoon, and then places the egg in the bowl of the next player of his, or her, team. So it goes, until all of the players of one team have successfully completed the trip across the room before the players of any other team.

If an egg is dropped in transit, the player who drops it must pick it up and place it back on the bowl of his spoon before advancing farther.

15. Equine Laundry Race

A good whip, as they used to be called in the grand old horse-and-buggy days, will certainly favor this equine entertainment, which is participated in by couples, the girl acting the part of the horse and the man serving as the driver. As many couples may play at one time as space permits.

The couples line up at one end of the room. Each girl, after being blindfolded, is harnessed with ribbon or stout cord, slipping the ribbon around the back of her neck, over her shoulders, and under her arms, and is given two clothespins and a handkerchief, which she holds in her hands.

At the other end of the room is strung a clothesline, not too taut, and between the clothesline and the couples are placed a few chairs, in such a manner that each couple will be confronted by the same number of chairs to pass.

Now the men take the reins of their respective horses, and, at the signal to go, drive their horses (guiding them by pulling on the reins, as they would guide real horses) around the obstacles to the clothesline, where the horses, guided again by the tugging on their reins, hang their handkerchiefs on the clothesline, using both clothespins, and are then driven back to the starting line.

The first couple returning to the starting point after successfully hanging their laundry wins a bar of soap.

This is a good game for indoors or outdoors.

16. The Feather Game

Here is a lively game you can play according to your own rules. The simplest way to play it is to divide your guests into two teams and seat the teams on opposite sides of a long table. In the center of the table place a small feather. Now the object of the game is for each team to try to blow the feather off the opposite side of the table. The team which succeeds in doing this scores one point and the feather is replaced in the center of the table and the fun begins again. During play, hands must be kept under the table.

A more strenuous method of playing is to use a large blanket or sheet. Have your guests lie on their backs in a circle with their legs extended towards the center of the circle. Now cover them with the blanket and instruct each player to hold the edge of the blanket with his two hands, as close to his neck as possible. When all are so arranged, place the feather in the center of the blanket and give the signal for everyone to start blowing. The object of the game is now for each player to prevent the feather from coming to rest over his body and to try to force it to land on some other player's body. When a feather alights on a player that player is penalized one point. Also, if a player blows the feather off the blanket onto the floor, he is penalized one point.

83

17. Flicking Cards

When you were young, did you ever flick pieces of pasteboard so that they would soar, while rotating with great rapidity, across the room, usually the classroom? It was fun. So is this game which is based on the same principle.

Place a small scrapbasket, or an empty box, on the floor in the center of the room, and around this place four chairs, each about 6 or 7 feet from the scrapbasket. Seat two couples in these chairs and give each player a pack of cards, the newer the better. Of course, the packs of cards should have backs of different designs or colors. At a signal, the players begin flicking their cards, one at a time, at the scrapbasket. The player who gets the greatest number of his cards into the scrapbasket wins.

The players must at all times sit well back in their chairs. It is not "cricket" to sit on the very edge of the chair, lean forward, and stretch your arm out as far as you can.

If it is so desired, the cards in the scrapbasket may be scored according to their face values, counting fifteen for each ace, and ten for each of the face cards. Each couple should be partners and combine their scores. After all have played the game, various couples will be sure to challenge each other, but don't let this go on too long, or you will soon find that the enthusiasts will be monopolizing all the play, and the others won't like it.

18. Flower Darts

Dart games are extremely popular with both children and adults, and there is no end to the variety of interesting, sporty, comical, or ingenious targets that can be designed. You can make a pretty and really challenging dart target by painting on thick composition board different flowers, each of which is enclosed in a circle 3 or 4 inches in diameter. There should be 12 circles and 4 different kinds of flowers, 3 flowers of each kind (see diagram).

Each player is supplied with three darts and he scores 5 points for every circle in which one of the darts lands;

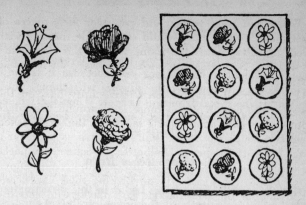

15 points if his darts land in two circles which enclose the same kind of a flower; 50 points if his darts land in three circles enclosing the same kind of a flower; 75 points if two darts land in the same circle; and 100 points if all three darts land in the same circle.

If darts are not available, rubber jar rings can be used instead, if in the center of each circle on the target a two-inch, right-angle hook is screwed. The object is to toss the jar rings over the hooks.

19. Guessing the Leader

A lively game for those to play who enjoy general confusion is this guessing game, which is guaranteed to cause confusion many times compounded.

The players sit in chairs arranged in a circle, facing inward. A Guesser is chosen and sent from the room. While the Guesser is out of the room, a Leader is chosen, and it is explained to the other players in the room that they must all follow instantly everything the leader does. The game begins by the leader's clapping his hands. The other players in the circle instantly clap their hands. This is the signal for the Guesser to return to the room and take a position in the center of the circle. Then the Leader, when he thinks the Guesser is not looking at him, stops clapping his hands and stamps his feet, and, of course, all the other players seated in the circle instantly do likewise. The Leader may then pat his head with his hands, wave his arms in the air, jump up and down, grunt, or perform any act he wants, and the others follow his lead. It is up to the Guesser to discover who does the leading. This is not easy, because it is quite remarkable how quickly the players will change their actions at the signal from the Leader. When the Leader is finally identified by the Guesser, he becomes the Guesser, and a new Leader is selected.

20. Hoop Relay Race

If you don't like the hoop factor in this diverting entertainment, substitute for the hoops cardboard squares, pie pans, blocks of wood, coverless shoeboxes, or anything else that strikes your fancy. You will have just as much fun with one as with another.

Divide your guests into teams of four or six members each. Half of the members of each team stand at one end of the room, and the other half stand at the other end of the room. To the first player of each team give two small hoops, not larger than 15 inches in diameter. At the signal to start, the first player of each team places one of his hoops on the floor in front of him, and then with his left foot steps into the hoop, raising his right foot from the ground and holding it off the ground. Now, balancing himself on his left foot, he places his second hoop on the floor in front of him, and with his right foot steps into that hoop, and then balances on his right foot while he turns, picks up his first hoop, and advances it along the floor towards the opposite side of the room. When, progressing in this manner, he reaches the opposite end of the room, he picks up his rear hoop and hands it to the second player on his team, who, stepping with his left foot into the hoop on the floor just vacated by the first player, starts back across the room in the same manner as his teammate managed the first crossing. As soon as the last player of any team completes the trip across the room, the race ends, and his team is declared winner.

If any player, during his progress across the room loses his balance and falls or touches the floor with either hand or the foot that is supposed to be off the floor, he must pick up both of his hoops and start his trip over again.

21. Horse Racing

This game, which invariably draws the biggest crowds on board passenger vessels, where it is regularly played, is always enjoyed at home parties when it is introduced, which is not as often as it should be.

It requires some equipment, but nothing difficult to procure or make. First there is a race track. This may be a sheet of paper 36″ wide and 9′ long. This paper

should have drawn on it with crayon or paint, 17 lines, 6 inches apart, running across the 36 inch width of the paper; and five lines, six inches apart, running the 9 foot length of the paper. The first crosswise line should be 6 inches from the edge of the paper and parallel with it. The first lengthwise line should be 6 inches from the edge of the paper and parallel with it. The 6th and the 12th crosswise lines should be double lines. Your track should look somewhat like the diagram above.

The double lines show where the hurdles belong. Hurdles can easily be made out of wood; or curtain rods, or canes resting on books will serve the purpose.

You must provide six "horses." These may be different

toy animals—stuffed dogs, cats, mice, etc.—or, if you are clever, you can make toy horses yourself out of wood, cardboard, or cloth. The sillier they are, the more entertainment they will provide.

You will also have to have two dice of different colors, say white and red; a dice cup; and plenty of small slips of paper.

When you have all this equipment in order, you are ready to play the game.

Place the race track on the floor and arrange the hurdles in their proper places. Line up the six horses in the first row of spaces across the track. The horses should be numbered from one to six, and each should have its number attached to him or painted on him.

The players then place their bets, by each buying a ticket for one chip for the horse he bets will win the race. The ticket is one of the slips of paper on which the banker writes down the number of the race and below that the number of the horse.

When all bets have been placed, one of the company throws the dice and calls the result. The red die shows the number of the horse and the white die shows how many spaces he is to move forward. If the red die showed 4 and the white die 3, horse number four would move three spaces ahead.

If a horse lands on a space directly before either hurdle, or double line, he cannot continue until the dice thrower calls a one for him. If a one is not called for a horse in such a position, the horse is not moved and the dice are thrown again.

A horse to finish the race must have called for him the exact number required to put him across the last line on the track. If he was in the third space from the end of the track, and the thrower called four for him, he could not be moved. If the call was two, he would be moved two spaces. To finish the call would have to be three.

At the end of the race, all of the chips paid in for bets are divided equally among the persons holding slips for the winning horse. Your guests should be permitted to take turns throwing dice and moving the horses.

22. House Treasure Hunt

There is an interesting and entertaining way of treasure hunting in your own home.

Collect twenty odd articles and make a written list of them. Then place them around the rooms in which your guests will be entertained, where they will be visible but not too obvious. A small, white lady's handkerchief, for instance, could be folded and pinned to a white window curtain; an eraser could be balanced beside the candle in a candle stick on a mantel; a pair of shears could be laid across the tops of the books in a bookcase; an air-mail postage stamp could be inserted in the corner of a picture frame hanging on the wall; a small vial of perfume could be placed next to the lock on a window frame; and so on.

Give each guest a copy of the list and instruct him to write on it the location of each article he has seen. No article may be moved or touched, and, of course, no treasure hunter should reveal to another the location of any of the articles he has seen.

A time limit of not more than 20 minutes should be imposed, in which the guests are to wander around the rooms in search of the treasures, and the first guest to return his list with correct notations tellings the locations of all of the articles, or at the end of the time limit has the greatest number of correct notations on his list, is the winner.

23. Jackass Relay Race

This is a team game and is played on a long table, preferably highly polished. Half of each of two teams line up, single file, at one end of the table, and the other half at the other end of the table. Two jackasses, cut from very light cardboard (see diagram below), are placed at one end of the table, one jackass in front of the lead-off man of each team. Each lead-off man is given a fan, and, at the signal to go, commences to fan his jackass across the table. When a jackass reaches the end of the table, the fanner hands his fan to his team-

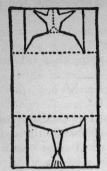

mate at the end of the table, who then turns the jackass around, and fans him back to the starting point, where the next player takes over the fan, and continues the race. The first team successfully to maneuver its jackass across the table the required number of times (once for each member of the team) wins this exciting contest.

If a jackass is fanned off the side of the table, the player responsible must pick it up, take it back to his end of the table, and continue the race from there.

24. Loud and Low

This is a variation of the old game called Hot and Cold. It is more fun because it is noisier and requires somewhat more skill in manipulating the signals.

One player is sent from the room, while the others decide upon something they want him to do on his recall, such as pick up a particular object off a particular table; sit down in a particular chair; turn on (or off) the radio; or even kiss the girl everyone knows he would like to kiss.

When the player returns another player guides his actions by beating on the bottom of a saucepan with a metal spoon. If the first player moves toward the object he is to touch, let's say the girl he is to kiss, the second player taps loudly on the pan; but if the first player moves away from the object, the second player taps more and more softly on the pan. The nearer the first player comes to doing what he is supposed to do, the louder the second player drums. Throughout the proceedings no words are spoken.

A really clever pan drummer can lead a person to do almost anything desired. Of course, some players respond more quickly to the pan-tapping than others.

25. Lunatic's Exchange

The lunatic who thought up this idea probably came to no good end, and it is possible that you will fare no better if you employ it. You do so at your own risk; but it will be worth the risk if you are sure that all of your guests are mentally sound, even-tempered, and not inclined to hysterics.

The idea is to inform each invited guest that he is to bring to your party, daintily wrapped as if it were a gift, the one thing in his possession with which he is heartily fed up and for which he has no earthly use. It may be anything, a white elephant, a useless and unwanted gift from Great Aunt Susan, an inherited nicknack that has been accumulating dust for years, etc., etc.

Write on small pieces of paper the names of all your guests, one name on each piece of paper. Fold up the pieces of paper and shuffle them in a hat. When all of your guests have arrived, have one of them draw two names at a time from the hat, and announce the names. The two persons whose names are called then exchange their gift packages. Then two more names are drawn and called and the next two packages exchanged. When all the names have been drawn, give the signal to open the packages. After that anything can happen, when your guests discover what atrocious objects they have had palmed off on them.

26. The Match Box Race

For an opening number, to take the chill off the atmosphere, the Match Box race is a dependable activity, unless one or more Cyrano de Bergeracs happen to be among the guests, in which case it might be best to try something else.

The players are divided into two teams, with an equal number of men and women on each team. The teams are lined up facing each other, and in each team the positions of the men and women alternate. The first man on each team is given the cover of an ordinary, pocket-size, safetymatch box, into one end of which he must insert his nose sufficiently far to retain the cover on his nose without the aid of his hands. At the signal to start, each leader turns to the girl next to him on his team and transfers, without any help from his or her hands, the match-box cover from his nose to hers. She then turns to the man next to her in line and does likewise. So the match-box cover should proceed, from nose to nose, down the lines of both teams. The team which first gets its match-box cover in this manner to the nose of the last girl or man on its line wins.

If a match-box cover is dropped, it must be returned to the leader, who must start it down the line again, from nose to nose. After the match-box cover once begins its journey it may not be touched by any hands, unless it falls to the ground, when it may be picked up by the hands to be returned for a fresh start.

27. Match Building

A couple of boxes of kitchen matches and a bottle with a cork provide the materials for a very ticklish business that will give enjoyment to young and old alike for a considerable period of time.

Place the bottle, with the cork in its proper place, on a card table. Seat five or six persons around the table, and give each person an equal number of matches. Now sharpen to points the untreated end of four matches, and stick these matches upright into the cork in the bottle. Each person in turn then places a match between the matches stuck in the cork, in such a way as to balance the match on the cork. The players continue to add, one at a time, each in turn, as many matches as they can successfully balance on the construction. Every match knocked off the structure during the operation of adding a new match must be picked up by the person responsible and added to his supply of matches. The player who first exhausts his supply of matches, or who has the fewest number of matches left in his supply when the game is halted, is the winner.

In adding matches, the matches need not be balanced on top of the matches already played. Whenever it is possible, a match may be poked in between two or more other matches. The only requirements are that a match when placed must remain as placed and that in placing it no other match may be knocked off the structure without the penalty mentioned above. The players may use only one hand in placing matches, and no player may touch the bottle or the table.

It is quite surprising how high a structure can be built in this manner.

28. Match Striking

Here is a jolly game for pyromaniacs and had best be played on a breezeless beach free from inflammable accoutrements and where plenty of water is readily available for emergency use. It is an appropriate pastime for a Fourth of July party.

Provide each player with a packet of paper matches and explain that at the word Go he must try to light one at a time all the twenty matches in the packet, striking each match, *only once*, on the prepared surface of the match-packet cover. If a player strikes a match and it fails to light, he is immediately disqualified. The person wins who succeeds first in lighting all twenty of his matches, or who lights the greatest number of matches according to the rules.

If this game is played indoors, one or more pails of water should be provided into which the lighted matches are to be tossed. A fire extinguisher near at hand will be useful in dealing with the lighted matches that miss the pail and land on the Persian rug. This pastime may prove to be the last on your program, so, when planning the party, you might just as well schedule it for the final activity.

29. Meeting of Ghosts

This is a very amusing way to choose partners for games, supper, dancing, or any other purpose. For each of the men at your party write on a piece of paper the name of a well-known deceased male character known to have had a wife, and write before the name the words, *The Ghost of.* Fold these pieces of paper and shuffle them in a hat. For the girls, write on separate pieces of paper the names of the wives of the male characters you have selected for the men. If one of the male characters is known to have had more than one wife, only one wife's name may be used. Fold these pieces of paper and shuffle them in another hat.

When it comes time to choose partners, have each man take a name from the men's hat and each girl take a name from the girls' hat. They are to remember the names, but must not reveal them to each other. The girls are now blindfolded and told to find the ghosts of their husbands. When a girl locates a man, she asks him if he is the ghost of her husband, naming her husband or who she thinks is her husband. If he is the right ghost, he says, "Yes," and she says, "I am the ghost of your wife so-and-so" (giving the name she drew from the hat). She then takes off her blindfold and the two become partners. If the man is not the ghost of her husband, he says, "No," and she moves on.

In this game the ghost of Eve would seek the ghost of Adam; the ghost of Josephine would look for the ghost of Napoleon; and the ghost of Anne Hathaway would search for the ghost of Will Shakespeare.

30. Murder

If your house is provided with a fully equipped first-aid chest and the members of your party are followers of the strenuous life, you can have a really exciting time by playing Murder. But just remember that this is no game for the kiddies or for weak-hearted middle-agers.

First, provide as many small slips of paper as there are players. Then, on one of these slips write the word Detective and on another slip write the word Murderer.

After this fold up all the slips of paper, both the blank slips and the two on which you have written, and put them in a hat. When all the slips are in the hat, pass the hat among the players, and instruct each to draw one slip, look at it surreptitiously, and not let any one else know whether or not he has drawn a blank. When all the slips have been drawn from the hat only the murderer and the detective will know their identities and they must not reveal them. This is most important.

All the lights are now turned off in the several rooms in which the game is to be played. The players then silently move around in the dark, going whither they will. The murderer stealthily seeks a victim, who may be any one but the detective, who when the lights go off sits in a chair and waits for the crime to be committed. When the murderer thinks he has found a satisfactory victim, he suddenly places his hands around the victim's neck and very gently squeezes it. The victim then must scream his or her most blood-curdling scream and fall to the floor. Upon hearing the scream, the detective must leap to his feet and shout, "Lights!" At this command, the person nearest to the light-switch in the room where the murder takes place immediately switches on the lights. The detective goes to the scene of the crime and starts an investigation, questioning the several players in an effort to ascertain who is the murderer. All of the players excepting the murderer and the victim must answer the detective's questions truthfully. The murderer may answer truthfully or falsely. The victim must remain silent, as a well-behaved corpse should.

After the detective has identified the murderer or has admitted his inability to do so, the slips of paper are collected, shuffled again in the hat, and passed among the players for the selection of another murderer and detective. And crime marches on.

31. Number Race

There is a lot of fun to be had with this test of clear vision and quick observation and it can be heartily recommended as an entertaining diversion.

First prepare two large charts which should be identical, but need not be, by pasting on each in a confusing pattern a hundred numbers, cut from a large wall calendar or a daily desk calendar. Since only 31 different numbers are used in a calendar, there will be duplications on your charts, which is as it should be. The same numbers must appear on both charts, although their positions need not be the same on both charts. Of course, the numbers must not appear consecutively on the charts; they should be well mixed.

Divide your guests into two teams and have each stand in single file, about eight or ten feet in front of each chart, with their backs to the charts. Give the end person nearest the charts in each team a black crayon. Now a leader calls a number, and each of the two persons with the crayons must turn around, run up to his chart, find the number called, and mark on it an X, crossing it out. He then returns to his team and hands his crayon to his next team mate nearest the chart.

As soon as one of the first players crosses out the first number called, the leader calls a second number, without waiting for the other player to cross out the first number on his chart. The second number called is for the second players on each team to find and cross out as quickly as possible.

The object of the game is to see which team first crosses out all of the numbers called with the fewest mistakes. When a mistake is made, the person making the mistake must go back and correct it before the next player may play.

In playing this game, it is best for the leader to write down, before the game starts, the numbers he is going to call, in the order in which he is going to call them. Then there will be no arguments, after the game is over, as to who was expected to cross out what number.

As there is little doubt that your guests will want a second chance at this sport, you had better prepare in advance two or three sets of charts. But you will be well advised not to have the game played more than three times.

32. Numbered Chairs

There always comes a time when a host or hostess is confronted with the problem of entertaining a group of persons who enjoy activity just so long as it does not put too great a strain on their intellectual capacities. Variations of such pastimes as Going-To-Jerusalem, Bean Bag, Blindman's Buff, Advancing Statues, and the like are the usual solution to the problem. Another game that will appeal to such a group is Numbered Chairs, which really can be very amusing.

The players sit in a row of chairs and count off. Each chair then, throughout the game, retains its number, which is adopted by whoever sits in the chair. The game begins by the player who sits in chair number 1 calling out the number of another chair, say 5. The player who is sitting in chair 5 must immediately call another number, say 8. Whereupon the player on chair 8 shouts out a new number. This continues as rapidly as possible until some player fails to respond instantly to the number of the chair on which he sits, or another player responds out of turn. In that case the person making the error must move to the last chair on the line, and those players who occupy the intervening chairs must each move up one chair towards the head of the line. Confusion is caused by the fact that each time a player moves into a new chair, the number to which he must respond changes to that of the new chair. The faster the game is played, the more errors will be made, and the more frequently will the players be changing chairs. If the game is continued for any length of time, those who are easily confused, will undoubtedly become completely irrational.

33. Paper Barge Loading

Few persons know that a flat sheet of ordinary paper floated on water can hold a surprising number of articles and still remain afloat. The trick is to place on the paper a somewhat smaller sheet of stiff cardboard and on the cardboard place the articles. This is an exciting game, which can be played at a table or on the floor.

The first thing is to provide a large bowl or tub, filled with water. Only three or four inches of water will be necessary. The players sit around this bowl. The next thing is to have ready a number of sheets of ordinary wrapping paper, measuring 8″ by 6″ each; an equal number of sheets of stiff cardboard, measuring 7″ by 5″ each; and plenty of poker chips.

Now, very carefully, float on the water in the bowl a sheet of wrapping paper, being sure that none of its edges or corners is turned down. If the paper lies absolutely flat on the water, it will float, but no water should be allowed to come over the sides of the paper. On top of the floating paper, and centered, place a sheet of the stiff cardboard. This is the barge that is to be loaded with poker chips.

Divide the chips evenly among the players and instruct the players to place, each in turn, one chip on the barge. The object is to see how many chips can be placed on the barge without sinking it. The player whose chip sinks the barge, or who drops his chip into the water, or knocks any other chip off the barge into the water, must salvage the sunken cargo and add it to his supply of chips. A new barge is then floated and the game continues. The player who is first to exhaust all of his chips, or who, when the game is stopped, has the fewest number of chips in his possession, is the champion barge loader.

Inasmuch as the barges will rarely ever be loaded twice in exactly the same manner, it cannot be foretold when a barge will sink or topple into the water.

34. Parted Couples

An amusing way of starting off a party in the right spirit and of introducing the guests to one another is to prepare in advance as many cards (about 8″ x 4″) as there are to be persons present. These cards should be of two colors; one color for the men, and another color for the girls. To each card attach a piece of ribbon or colored string, so that the card may be hung from a person's neck. Now, on each of the cards for the men paint or crayon the name of a man in a well-known couple, such as Romeo, of the well-known Romeo and Juliet couple. On each of the cards for the girls paint or crayon the name of a female member of a couple; in this case, Juliet. For instance, the first man's card might have JACK, then the first girl's card would have JILL. The second man's card might have ANTHONY and the second girl's card must have CLEOPATRA. And so on.

Shuffle the men's cards and hang them together conveniently near where you will receive your guests as they arrive, and do the same with the cards for the girls. As the guests are received, hand to each one a card; the men, of course, each getting one of the men's cards, and the girls each getting one of the girls' cards. Each guest is instructed to hang the card from his or her neck and to go forth and seek the other member of the couple suggested by the name on the card. In this way the parted couples are brought together and should remain partners for the duration of the party.

A FEW WELL-KNOWN COUPLES

Jack and Jill	Adam and Eve	Anthony and Cleopatra
Leander and Hero	Tristan and Isolde	Burns and Allen
William and Mary	Samson and Delilah	Edward and Wally
Romeo and Juliet	Ike and Mamie	Punch and Judy
	Tex and Jinx	

35. Photographer

If you have utter confidence in your guests, and there are not too many of them, you may be bold enough to introduce this bit of high-jinks.

All the guests are asked to leave the room and await a call to participate in the game. The hostess then arranges, in one corner of the room, two straight-back chairs, side by side; and then calls for a gentleman and a lady to enter the room. She explains to them that they have just been married and they are to have their photograph taken. She then asks them to be seated and pose in a very grim and formal Victorian manner. When the couple are posed to her satisfaction, the hostess goes to the door and calls for another man. When he has entered, the door is closed behind him, and the hostess leads him to the bridal couple who are waiting to have their picture taken. She explains the situation to the newcomer, and tells him that he is the photographer who is to take the picture. Then she asks him what is wrong with the pose assumed by the couple. When he answers, she says, "Good. Now, you pose them as you think they should appear in their first picture together after their wedding."

The photographer then rearranges the couple to his liking. If he is a serious-minded young man he may tell them to relax, look at each other, and smile. If he is of a more frivolous nature he may tell them to hold hands and instruct the "bride" to put her head on the "groom's" shoulder and look "cute."

When the photographer has the couple arranged as he wants, the hostess orders him to take the place of the "husband," and to assume with the girl the exact same pose as he directed the girl and her previous "husband" to assume. That's the surprise.

Now a girl is called into the room. The situation is explained to her and she is urged to pose the couple as she thinks they ought to be. When she is satisfied with her pose, she must take the place of the "bride." So it goes until every guest has had an opportunity to pose the newly married pair.

You may be sure that each "photographer" will have a new suggestion to make. Both the poses and the reactions of the photographers, when they are told to substitute for the models, will never fail to drive the least suggestion of dull care from the minds of your guests.

36. Plate Spinning

For those who are alert and nimble this is a good game. The guests are seated in chairs arranged in a circle. One player is elected to be It. He goes to the center of the circle and is given a china or tin plate, or a piepan. This he must spin as vigorously as possible; and as soon as the plate begins to spin, he must call out the name of another player and then run to his own chair. If he seats himself in his own chair before the player whose name he has called catches the plate while it is still spinning, the player whose name was called becomes It and must spin the plate and call another name; otherwise, the first person remains It and must spin the plate again and call a new name. Each player who catches the spinning plate before It has seated himself in his own chair scores 5 points.

Contrary to the wishes of your guests, this game should be stopped before any one collapses. If you permit it to continue for more than 20 minutes, you do so at your own risk.

37. *Potato Racing*

The old fashioned potato race, which must be familiar to everyone, is best suited to the outdoors; but there is another kind of potato race, that is just as much fun, which can be enjoyed indoors.

At each end of the living room place two, three, or four chairs, depending on the width of the room. The chairs at one end of the room face the chairs at the other end. On each of the chairs at one end of the room place three large potatoes, and on each of the opposite chairs place a bowl.

Assign a guest to each of the chairs on which are the potatoes and give him a table knife. At the signal to begin, each participant must pick up a potato on the flat end of his knife, carry it across the room, and deposit it in the bowl on the chair opposite to the chair he started from. The first player to succeed in depositing his three potatoes in this fashion wins.

If a potato falls on the floor while in transit, it must be picked up with the knife. No hands are permitted to touch the potatoes after the race starts.

You can try the same thing, using eggs instead of potatoes, if you really don't give a toot about your furniture and rugs.

38. Sardines

For a party in a large country house this is the ideal game. The entire house, with the exception of the kitchen, pantry, and dining room, perhaps, should be thrown wide open to the guests, and not a ray more of light should be permitted than safety makes absolutely necessary.

All of the guests assemble in one room and remain there for two or three minutes while a selected couple go forth quietly and hide themselves together somewhere in the house. At the end of the two or three minutes, the other couples set out in search of the hidden pair. The first couple to locate the hidden pair join the hidden pair in their hideaway without making any sound whatever. As each succeeding couple discover the hideaway, they too silently join the occupants. You can well believe that before the last couple has found the hiding place its occupants will literally be packed in like sardines in a can. The first couple to locate the hiders are entitled to do the hiding next time.

Impress upon the players the need for absolute quiet while playing the game. Laughing, giggling, whispering will surely spill the beans.

39. Siamese Racing

If you are looking for something to provide fun during a picnic, beach party, or garden party, this activity will do the trick. It is a first rate pastime for dispelling all feelings of social inadequacy and shyness.

This sport is a race between couples who run back-to-back. The partners stand at the starting line, each couple back-to-back, with their arms interlocked, the man facing the halfway line, some forty or fifty feet away, the ladies, of necessity, facing in the opposite direction. At the signal to start, the couples, without disengaging their arms, run—no walking, please— to the halfway line, the men, naturally, running forward, and the ladies, poor dears, being forced to run backwards. At the halfway mark the procedure is reversed, and the ladies run forward, with the men running backwards, until they have returned to the starting line. The first couple back over the starting line with their arms still interlocked win, whether still on their feet, or not. The disengagement of arms is cause for disqualification.

This is one of those pastimes that provide as much fun for the spectators as for the participants.

40. Slap Jack

Here is a very good outdoor game indeed, but must not be indulged in by cardiac patients.

All the players excepting It stand in a circle, facing inwards, with their hands held open behind their backs. It is given a rolled-up newspaper, or a light switch. With this weapon in his possession he circles around the backs of the players, and then suddenly places the weapon in the hands of one of the players. The instant he does this, he must run like everything until he has completely encircled the players and has returned to the place where he disposed of the weapon. In the meantime, the player who has taken possession of the weapon gives chase, and must try to belabor It with the weapon as often as he can. If It succeeds in getting around the circle and occupying the place vacated by the player who is chasing him without being hit, the chaser becomes It, otherwise It remains It for another turn.

41. Streamer Cutting

Racing games can always be counted on to enliven a party, and this is one of the liveliest and most amusing of the racing games for indoor sport.

Provide each couple with a one-inch-wide paper streamer, 8 feet long, and a pair of scissors. The men line up at one end of the room, each holding one end of a streamer. The girls form a line facing their partners, as far from their partners as the lengths of the streamers will permit. The girls have the scissors, and at a given signal they start cutting their streamers lengthwise. The first one who succeeds in cutting her streamer in half

103

from the end she originally held to the end held by her partner wins. The cutting should be continuous. Any contestant who cuts through the edge of her streamer is immediately disqualified and must withdraw from the race.

After the girls have had their chance, new streamers should be distributed and the men should be permitted to do the cutting while the girls hold the streamers. Then the girls may race the men, half the girls and men cutting at the same time, then the other half, and finally the winners of the two heats.

Instead of having the players hold the streamers, the goal ends of the streamers can be pinned to the back of a sofa or to the backs of chairs arranged in a row, or can be fastened with thumb tacks to a mantel shelf, a book shelf, window sill, or some other practical object. In which case, the cutters must be careful not to pull the streamers loose from their anchorages, which is cause for the disqualification of the careless contestant.

42. Tiddlywinks Baseball

Grown-ups like to play on the floor just as children do. And it is good for their souls occasionally to get down from the high places and act lowly. You can't be lofty, dignified, and condescending while crawling around on all fours. And crawling around on all fours is just what is expected from you in this game, which is played by two teams of two or three players each.

With white tape (or French chalk) lay out on the floor the two foul lines of a baseball diamond. About 3 feet from the juncture of these lines (Home Plate) on the right field line, place a teacup. At the juncture of the foul lines place a small white tiddlywink, which represents the baseball, and beside it place a small colored tiddlywink, which represents the base runner.

The players on the team which is In the Field, kneel on the floor in the outfield, facing Home Plate. Each holds in one hand a teacup and in the other a large tiddlywink (or shooter). One of the players on the other team, which is At Bat, kneels on the floor near the Home Plate and holds a large tiddlywink in his hand. Now everything is in readiness to start the game.

The player at Home Plate snaps the baseball (white tiddlywink), endeavoring to make it go as far as possible within the foul lines and trying to keep it from soaring too high in the air. The instant he snaps the baseball, he turns his attention to the base runner, and, by snapping him with his shooter, he rushes him to the teacup on the foul line (First Base) and tries to get him into the teacup. Meanwhile the fielders try to catch the baseball in one of their teacups, if the white tiddlywink has been snapped high, or else one of the fielders, as soon as the baseball has come to rest, begins to snap it towards First Base. If the fielder gets the baseball into the First Base teacup before his opponent gets the base runner (colored tiddlywink) into the First Base teacup, the base runner is counted out, otherwise he is safe and there is one man on base. If the fielder catches the baseball in his teacup before it touches the floor, the base runner is counted out.

After the play has been concluded, the second player of the team At Bat kneels on the floor near the Home Plate and snaps the baseball and then the base runner, and the fielders carry on as before.

Men on bases advance one base only every time a base runner is safe at First Base, so a score is made only after four base runners have reached First Base safely before three have been declared out.

After three base runners have been declared out at First Base, the teams change positions, and the game is continued in this manner for as many innings as desired.

An important rule is that the players must not interfere with each other. Both the fielder and the player with the base runner must have free access to the First Base cup.

43. Tightrope Racing

If you want to get some idea of how a tightrope walker feels the first time he risks his neck on the high wire, just try to walk along a straight line looking through the large lenses of a pair of opera glasses. It's quite a sensation, and, further more, it's quite an entertaining sight for whoever may be a witness to your experiment.

For fun at a party, stretch three lengths of white tape, each about twelve feet long, across the floor of the room, pining them down to the rug or thumb-tacking them to the floor. The tapes should run parallel and be about three or four feet apart. These represent tightropes. Now have each of three guests stand at one end of each tape, with both feet on the tape, the heel of the right shoe touching the toe of the left shoe.

As they balance thus, hand each of the three guests a pair of opera glasses and tell him to focus them on his "tightrope" while looking through the big lenses. Tell all that at the signal to start they are to race to the ends of the "tightropes." The only rules are, first, they may not take their eyes away from the large lenses of the glasses; and, two, they must not step off the tape. Breaking either of these rules results in instant disqualification.

Give the signal to start and watch the fun. Permit every one to do this stunt, and have those who succeed in getting to the ends of their tapes compete for a grand prize.

44. Touch the Third

In a book of games written over a hundred years ago, this lively game is called Tierce, or Touch the Third, and is said to afford "charming exercise."

All but one couple stand in a circle, two deep. The remaining couple stands outside the circle, a reasonable distance apart. One member of this couple is the Pursuer and the other is the Pursued. At a signal the Pursuer pursues the Pursued in an effort to touch him. At no time may the Pursued enter the circle excepting to escape the Pursuer; and as soon as he enters the circle he must take a stand in front of one of the couples. When he does this he makes the circle at this point three deep, which may not be, so the extra person on the outside of the circle at this point immediately becomes the

Pursued and must in turn try to escape from the Pursuer, by dashing into the circle and standing in front of another couple.

If the Pursuer touches the Pursued, the Pursued then becomes the Pursuer, and the former Pursuer becomes the Pursued. This is really a good game for those who want plenty of action. It is most fun when played outdoors.

45. Turtle Racing

Races of almost any kind—excepting the early morning race to catch the 7:31 Commuters' Special—can be counted on to provide fun, and this turtle race is one of the best for the purpose. It requires some skill but can be learned quickly with very little practice.

The first thing is to obtain several racing turtles. This is accomplished with the aid of a pencil, a pair of shears (or a sharp knife), and some cardboard or Bristol board. The turtles are drawn on the cardboard (see diagram on next page) and then cut out. The important things about these racing turtles are, first, the bottoms of the rear feet and the tip of the tail must be aligned; and, second, a hole must be punctured through the center of each head. You can have as many turtles as you wish, but they must all be exactly alike in every respect.

When you have obtained the turtles, place at one end of the room, in a row, as many kitchen chairs as you have turtles. To the top rung of each chair tie a string, about 12 feet long. About 3 feet directly in front of each chair place two large books, one on top of the other. About 8 feet in front of these books, or hurdles, pin to the rug or carpet a length of white tape, to indicate the starting line for the race.

Now place the turtles at the starting line, one directly in front of each chair, so that the two rear feet and the tip of the tail of each turtle touches the white tape. Through the hole in the head of each turtle thread the string that is attached to the chair in front of the turtle. Each player is then assigned a different turtle, and he takes up in his hand the free end of the string upon which his turtle hangs. Raising the string, he makes his turtle stand on its hind feet, which are touching the starting line. The players should be warned not to make their turtles stand too straight. Each turtle should incline slightly towards his chair.

When all the players are in readiness, the signal to start is given. Each player then relaxes his string sufficiently to allow his turtle to fall forward a few inches. He then tightens the string, by pulling it towards him. This movement raises the turtle's head again and at the same time moves its hind legs forward along the floor.

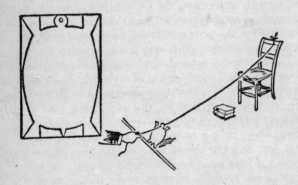

By repeating this procedure over and over again, relaxing and tightening the string, the player can make his turtle move with considerable rapidity towards the chair.

When the turtle reaches the hurdle (books), the player must raise his string in such a way as to balance the turtle on his hind legs on top of the books. He then continues the relaxing and tightening procedure and moves the turtle about a foot beyond the books.

When the turtle has passed beyond the hurdle, the player, by jiggling the string, tightening and relaxing it quickly, makes the turtle change its direction, its body inclined towards the starting line instead of towards the chair. The object now is to bring the turtle back, over the hurdle, to the starting line, employing the same procedure of relaxing and tightening the string used previously.

The manipulator of the first turtle to return to the starting line wins the race.

In manipulating the turtles, each player should take care to keep his turtle inclined in the direction it is supposed to be going. Too sudden or strong a jerk on the string will flip a turtle over, and, obviously, change its direction.

This game is not nearly so difficult to play as it is to describe, and it is well worthwhile experimenting with it. Once you have familiarized a group with its technique, you will have a hard time persuading the players to change to another pastime.

46. Up Jenkins!

This old favorite has all the elements that make up the perfect game. It requires some skill, demands close attention, has plenty of action, is exciting, and is frequently laugh-provoking.

The players are divided into two teams, which are seated on opposite sides of a long bare table. A quarter is provided and is tossed to see which team gains possession of it. The two opposing players nearest the head of the table are the first two opposing captains and only their orders are to be followed. Other players may give orders, but their orders must not be obeyed.

Now all the players of the team possessing the quarter place their hands under the table and pass the quarter from one to another, taking care not to reveal at any time to the opposing players the whereabouts of the quarter. The captain of the opposing team calls, "Jenkins says, Hands up." At that specific command, worded exactly that way, all the players on the team which has the quarter, bring their hands up from under the table and rest their elbows on the table, with their arms perpendicular to the table and their fists closed. Now the opposing captain calls, "Jenkins says, Hands down!" At this command, worded exactly that way, all the players, simultaneously, drop their hands, palms downward, fingers extended, on the table. In doing this they slap the table, with the flat of their hands, to make enough noise to drown the clink of the coin as it comes against the table absolutely still, while the opposing team tries to eliminate all the hands *excepting* the one under which the quarter rests. The opposing players may advise their captain, but the orders of the captain only are to be obeyed. He will say to a player on the team which has the quarter, "Jenkins says, Take away your right hand." The player does as he is told, and, if the quarter is not in view, the opposing captain tells another player what hand Jenkins says to take away. This continues until the quarter is discovered.

The team which holds the quarter scores 1 point for each hand still on the table at the time the quarter is discovered. If all of the hands have been ordered removed from the table excepting the one which hides the quarter, then the quarter is given to the opposing team and no score is made. The opposing team now has the quarter and must obey the orders of the captain of the team that no longer has the quarter.

A few rules and recommendations for this game must be emphasized:

1. The orders must be given correctly before they may be obeyed. "Jenkins says, Hands up" must be obeyed when called by the captains. But "James says, Hands up!" must never be obeyed, no matter who says it. If a player follows a wrong order given by anyone, or a correct order given by a player other than the captains, his team must forfeit the quarter without scoring.

2. No rings should be worn on the fingers of the players, excepting of course wedding rings, which some persons never remove.

3. The table upon which the game is played must be without a tablecloth or other covering.

4. Thirty seconds is all that should be allowed a team for passing the quarter to and fro under the table.

5. Each time a team regains the quarter, a new captain should be appointed, so that during the course of the game every one will have a chance of being captain.

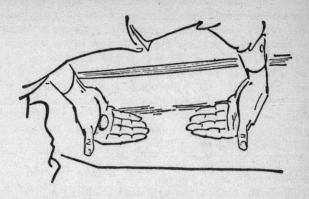

6. No one player should be permitted to monopolize the quarter when it is in the possession of his team. Every player should have a chance of holding the quarter at one time or another.

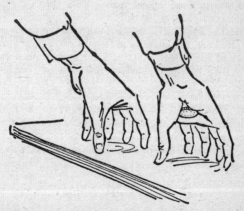

There are many ways of bringing the hands down to the table, some of which are for the experts only and require almost the skill of a magician. Here are a few that you may want to try.

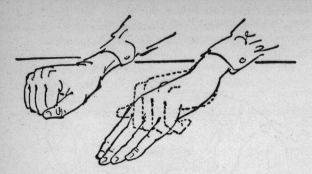

The order: Jenkins says, Grand slam!

Execution: The hands are brought down as described previously only with great force and much noise.

The order: Jenkins says, Fences!

Execution: The hands are brought down cautiously in front of the player with the fingers extended and the palms facing toward the player, the hands forming right angles with the forearms. The thumbs must be above the fingers, so that they can be seen. The person who has the quarter holds it pinched in his palm. The others hold their hands as if a quarter was pinched in their palms. (See illus.)

The order: Jenkins says, Dance!

Execution: The hands are brought down with the palms parallel to the table and the fingers and thumbs extending downward, like a lot of spider legs. The tips of the fingers touch the table and the fingers are wiggled in imitation of dancing legs. (See illus.)

The order: Jenkins says, Creepy Crawley!

Execution: The closed fists are brought down to the table with the knuckles up and the heel of the palm touching the table. Now comes the difficult part. The fingers are very cautiously unbent and extended until the entire hand is flat, palm down, on table. (See illus.)

47. *What's My Name?*

This is an excellent ice-breaker and a good pastime to keep the early guests occupied while they are waiting for the late arrivals. On as many small sheets of paper as there are to be guests at your party write different names of famous persons. As each guests arrives pin one of these sheets of paper on his or her back and tell each person to find out by questioning others who he or she is. The questions must be answered only by "Yes" or "No."

Let us say Sally Jones arrives and has pinned on her back the name J. Fred Muggs. She sees on the back of Charlie Pinkas the name Margaret Truman. Her conversation with Charlie will start something like this:

Sally: Am I a woman?
Charlie: No. Am I a man?
Sally: No. Am I alive?
Charlie: Yes. Am I alive?
Sally: Yes. Do I live in the United States?
Charlie: Yes. Do I live in the United States?
Sally: Yes. Am I an actor?
Charlie: Yes. Am I a pin-up girl?
Sally: No. Am I in the movies?
Charlie: No. Am I an author?
Sally: Yes. Am I on TV?
Charlie: Yes. Have I written a bestseller?
Sally: No. Am I a star?
Charlie: Yes. Do I write fiction?

and so it will go on until both have discovered their identities.

48. Who Is the Ghost?

This is an especially suitable game for Hallowe'en and other eerie occasions, and also offers an interesting method of picking partners.

The men leave the room and, while they are absent, the girls seat themselves on chairs and each is completely covered with a sheet. The men then return, and each goes to a different "ghost." Each man's problem now is to identify his ghost. To aid in doing this, he may ask the ghost to groan, boo, hiss, meow, whistle, cough, sigh, or make some other sound, and she must do so. He may also pass his hands over the ghost's head and facial features, outside the sheet. The ghost at no time is to speak.

When a man guesses the identity of the ghost, she comes out from under the sheet, and becomes his partner. If a man fails to identify the first ghost he encounters, he swaps ghosts with another man who has been equally unsuccessful, and tries again. Not more than two or three minutes should be allowed for identification. After that period the men who have not made an identification try their luck with another ghost, for another two minutes. So it goes until all the ghosts have been recognized, or until there is no further opportunity for the unsuccessful men to move to a new ghost. When the game ends, each of the poor fellows who have not been bright enough to identify any of the ghosts takes for a partner the last ghost he tried to identify; and, who knows, she may prove to be the prettiest and cleverest lady of them all.

This game very likely will merit an encore, in which case, try it again, reversing the procedure—send the girls out of the room and put the men under the sheets.

49. Who Is Your Neighbor?

For the glee club enthusiasts this game is just the thing.

The guests are divided into two teams. While Team A is out of the room, the members of Team B are blindfolded and seated on chairs arranged in a circle, with an unoccupied chair next to each player. When Team B is so arranged, the members of Team A come very quietly into the room and seat themselves on the unoccupied chairs, and, at a signal from their captain, all sing together a song agreed to among themselves when they were out of the room. Now it is up to each member of Team B to identify by the sound of his or her singing voice his neighbor on his right or left.

As soon as a person identifies one of his neighbors, he removes his blindfold and joins in the song. If any neighbors are still to be identified after the song is finished, the song may be repeated. Then Team B leaves the room and the members of Team A takes over the blindfolds and the alternate chairs.

The performance of the two teams may be timed, and the team which is quickest in identifying all of its neighbors wins. If neither team is successful in identifying all the neighbors, then the team wins which identifies the largest number of neighbors.

50. Who's Next?

This is a game that should be played at high speed. Let there be no hesitating or hemming and hawing, and soon your guests will be so muddled they won't be able to tell their right hand from their left, and will have forgotten the names of their best friends.

Seat the guests in a circle. Whoever is to start the game, suddenly points a finger at one of the seated guests, and mentioning his first name asks, "Who is next?" Now, here is the catch. If the leader points with his right hand, the player pointed at must immediately point to some other player *on his right*, and call his or her name. If the leader points with his left hand, the player pointed at must point to another player *on his left*. The second player may point with either his right or left hand.

The game will proceed like this. James points with his right hand at Mary, and says: "Mary, who's next?" Mary points with her *left hand* at George, who is on her *right*, and says, "George." George instantly points with his *right hand* at Rebecca, who is on *his left*, and says, "Rebecca." Rebecca mixes things up by pointing with her *right hand* at Armitage, who is on *her right*, and says, "Armitage." And so the game goes.

The action must be quick. Any player who hesitates, or hems or haws, or who fails to say correctly the first name (no nicknames are permitted) of the player at which he points is charged with a demerit.

51. Wink

This game, which was enjoyed by great-grandma and great-grandpa in the days of hoop-skirts, high hats, chaperons, and stifling conventions, is just as popular with uninhibited moderns as it was with great-grandma and great-grandpa, and is an excellent amusement to introduce at an engagement party, or a bridal shower, or a birthday party for one of the younger set.

As many chairs as there are men participating are arranged in a circle, facing inwards. All but one of these chairs are then occupied by the girls of the party. The hostess, or a volunteer, acts as umpire. Back of each chair, including the vacant chair, stands a man. He must stand at attention with his hands at his sides.

When all are so arranged, the "wolf" who is standing behind the vacant chair looks directly at one of the beauties sitting in the circle and winks at her with a wicked leer. As soon as this signal is given, the lady winked at must immediately endeavor to abandon her companion and rush to her new boy friend and occupy his chair. Her companion must try to restrain her by quickly clutching and holding her by her shoulders the instant she starts to move.

If the lady winked at is quick and agile enough to escape from her companion, her companion then becomes the wolf and will have to fill his vacated chair by winking at some other beauty. However, if the companion succeeds in preventing the escape of his winked-at lady, then the original wolf must try again to fill his vacant chair by the winking procedure.

It is important that the following rules governing this game be explained and strictly enforced. First, the gentlemen must stand like gentlemen, with their hands at their sides; and, second, they may not move their hands until the wolf has ogled and the object of his attention has made some motion.

After no more than twenty minutes of playing this game have the girls and men change places.

For rewards, each person who succeeds in occupying the wolf's chair may demand a forfeit from the wolf, or may be given 5 points to be added toward his or her accumulated score. The same rewards should go to each who is successful in preventing his companion's escape. If a forfeit, the forfeit is paid by the would-be escaper to the one who prevented the escape.

52. *Word Hunt*

This hunting game, like several of the other hunting games in this book, provides a means of keeping your early guests pleasantly occupied until the last tardy guest appears.

The best way to explain how to prepare in advance for this game is first to describe how the game is played. As each guest arrives he is given a card or slip of paper on which is written: "Your word has six letters, each of which is numbered 1 (or whatever number it may be)." The guest is told to find the letters with the correct numbers, which are hidden somewhere about the room. When a guest finds all six letters with his number on them, he must discover what word the letters spell. The first guest to find all his letters and discover his word wins.

Before the party begins, make up a list of as many six-letter words as you expect guests to be at the party. Then, on colored cards, about 3 x 5 inches in size, draw with crayon, or paint, all the letters used in your list of words, having only one letter on each card. Now number the cards, so that all of the letters which are required to spell the first word on your list are numbered 1; all of the letters required to spell the second word are numbered 2; etc. For example, if your first word is FRIEND, there will be six cards numbered 1, on each of which will be one of the six letters F, R, I, E, N, and D. If the second word is JESTER, there will be six cards numbered 2, on each of which will be one of the six letters J, E, S, T, E, and R.

All of the cards are shuffled and then hidden about the room or rooms in which the party is to be given.

4. Dramatic Games

53. Charades

THE CHARADE dates back to antiquity, and has had a most interesting development. It all goes back to Biblical times and the asking of riddles (Judges 14:8-18). A riddle is a question or statement so worded as to require considerable ingenuity in discovering its meaning.

From the riddle developed the charade, which originally was a riddle in verse. Then some one thought of proposing a riddle in pantomime. Instead of orally asking the riddle, a person, without speaking, tried by his actions alone to communicate what the riddle was. Later several people tried to communicate a riddle by silently acting together or by forming a tableau. Later conversation was introduced, and a riddle was acted like a very brief stage play, or skit, with words spoken. Then the game was not limited just to riddles, but employed single words, maxims, proverbs, or quotations. Then the persons who tried to communicate a word, maxim, proverb, or quotation, were not only allowed to speak, but could also use properties such as costumes, furniture, etc. Not only that, they were permitted to act out the word or words syllable by syllable.

Recently a new form of charades was developed in England, the popularity of which quickly spread to the United States, where it has won so great a following that it is now played on television programs as well as in the home.

This new form of charades is called The Game. In The Game one person acts the charade (a word, riddle, maxim, proverb, or quotation) by himself, entirely in pantomime, but he is permitted to use certain conventional gestures known to all the participants and which will help them in guessing what it is he is trying to communicate.

The Game: There are many variations of The Game, and each group that plays it has its own rules. Although it is often played by two teams, each of which performs in a separate room, many prefer to play it with a group assembled in one room, where two or more teams perform in company with each other. What follows will describe this manner of playing The Game, when the participants are divided into two teams and play together in one room.

First of all an umpire and two captains are chosen. The duties of the umpire are, first, to see that the rules agreed upon are strictly enforced; and second, accurately to keep and record the time consumed by each team in the performance of its charade. He should of course be impartial, and his decisions on all matters must be accepted as final.

After the umpire and the two captains have been chosen, the two teams are selected. This may be done in any of a number of ways. If there are as many ladies as men present, the ladies may be selected for one team, and the men for the other; or the captains may, alternating, each choose what players he wants for his team; or the teams may be chosen by lot.

When the teams have been chosen, each captain takes his team out of earshot of the other team, and in collaboration with his teammates selects as many words, sentences, maxims, proverbs, or quotations as there are members of the other team. When the items, which we shall hereafter call the charades, have been selected, each is written on a separate piece of paper, which is folded to hide the writing.

It may be required, and often is, that the charades selected by each team must in some way be related to each other. For example, all the charades selected by one team may have to do with dogs, such as

> The dog is man's best friend
> The little dog laughed to see such sport
> Love me, love my dog

Or they may concern one topic, such as love, war, sports, etc.; or be from the writings of one person—Shakespeare, Lincoln, Winston Churchill, etc. The point is that there must be a recognizable link between all the charades selected by a team.

When the charades have been chosen and written on pieces of paper, the folded pieces are given to the umpire, who must keep those selected by one team separate from those selected by the other team.

The game then really gets started by the umpire taking one of the charades selected by Team A and giving it to the captain of Team B. The captain of Team B then silently reads to himself the charade he has been given, keeping it a secret from his teammates. Having read it, he immediately begins to act it in complete silence. His teammates then try to guess as quickly as possible from his performance what the charade is. The umpire records the exact time it takes for Team B to guess the charade.

The performer, in this case the captain of Team B, may act the charade as a whole, or word for word, or the separate syllables in any one or more of the words. He is permitted also to act the words in any order he desires. But he must act speedily, in complete silence; and he may not use any "properties," either clothing or other objects. He may, however, point to any of his teammates or to any object in the room as an aid to indicating what he is trying to communicate. He may also employ the conventional gestures agreed upon to help him convey to his teammates the charade he is trying to interpret.

During his performance his teammates are permitted to ask any questions they wish; but the performer may reply only by the accepted gestures.

If the teammates are unable to guess the charade within ten minutes, or whatever time limit is set by the umpire, the charade is discarded and the team receives no score. If the team guesses the charade within the time limit, the umpire records on a tally sheet the exact time consumed.

The umpire then draws one of the charades chosen by Team B and presents it to the captain of Team A, who secretly reads it and then proceeds immediately to act it for the benefit of his teammates. As in the case of

Team B, the umpire records the time taken by Team A in guessing the charade acted by its captain.

The umpire then takes another charade chosen by Team A and hands it to a member of Team B other than the captain for him to act for his teammates. The game continues in this manner until every member of each team has acted a charade.

When all of the charades have been acted, the umpire adds up his tally sheets and announces which team has taken the least amount of time to guess its charades. That team is the winner.

The Conventional Gestures: Although different groups have their own rules, the following are among the most widely accepted conventional gestures used in The Game.

First off, the performer is required to indicate how many words there are in the charade he is to act. This he does by holding up his hand, or hands, and extending as many fingers as there are words. If there are more than ten words, he holds up both of his hands and extends all of his fingers and thumbs. He then closes his fists and, reopening them again, extends as many fingers as there are words over ten.

When he does this, one or more members of his team calls out the number for verification. The performer must then point a finger to any one who called the correct number and give the conventional gesture for "correct." This he does by crossing his hands, palms down, before his body, and then quickly uncrossing them and moving them away from each other towards the right and left on a line parallel to the floor. This gesture always means "right" or "correct."

To indicate "incorrect," the performer places his hands before his face, palms outward, fingers extended upwards, and then pushes them quickly away from his face.

After the performer has indicated the number of words in his charade, he must signal whether he will act the charade as a whole, act it word by word, or act one or more words syllable by syllable. If he elects to act the charade as a whole, he raises his right hand shoulder high and touches the tip of his right thumb

121

with the tip of his right index finger, forming a circle. This he holds in such a manner that all of his teammates can see it. One or more of his teammates then calls out, "The charade as a whole." The performer replies by giving the conventional gesture for "correct."

If the performer does not choose to perform the charade as a whole, he indicates which of the words in the charade he will act first. He does this with his fingers as before when indicated the total number of words in the charade. If he extends three fingers, that means he intends to act the third word in the charade. His teammates shout, "Third word" (or whatever it may be), and he must make the conventional gesture for "correct."

Should the performer fail, after two or three tries, to communicate to his teammates the word he is working on, he may decide to give it up temporarily and try another word. He indicates this by rapidly crossing and uncrossing his hands, palms out, in front of his face. This is the conventional gesture for "cross it out," "forget it," or "let's try something else." He then indicates with his fingers another word in the charade, the fifth or seventh or whatever he intends to act.

When the performer decides to do a word syllable by syllable, he signals which word he is to treat in that manner (first, second, third, etc.) and then with his right hand he pretends to chop his left arm into as many pieces as there are syllables in the word. This is the conventional gesture for informing the players that a word is going to be acted syllable by syllable and how many syllables there are in the word.

Certain very common words can very easily be indicated by obvious gestures. Man, gentleman, male, etc., is communicated by pointing a finger toward any man in the room. Likewise, woman, lady, girl, female, etc., is indicated by pointing a finger toward any girl in the room. The performer may point at or touch any part of his own body or the body of any teammate. He may also point at any inanimate object in the room. If he is trying to communicate the word *light*, he may point to a lamp or a light bulb. To point at himself means *me*. When he points at his eye he may mean *I* or *eye*.

Love is indicated by placing both hands over the heart. Any negative is indicated by shaking the head. *Better than, more than, greater than*, etc., are indicated by holding out the left hand and placing the right hand *above* it. *Less than, smaller than, worse than*, etc., are indicated by holding out the left hand and placing the right hand *under* it.

To indicate *opposite to*, the right index finger is pointed first to the right and then to the left. This gesture is used to inform a player that the correct word is the opposite of the word guessed. If the player had said "fat," he would immediately change it to "thin" or "slender."

The following are other useful gestures which all of the players should know.

Pointing a finger at the floor means *here, this place*.

Spreading the arms wide and then bringing the fingertips together in front of the body means *a lot, many, company, group*.

Forming a circle by crossing the wrists in front of the body and then diminishing the circle by bringing the left hand towards the right shoulder and the right hand towards the left shoulder means *a little, few, a small group*.

During the guessing, a near guess is considered to be warm or hot, depending on how close it comes to the correct answer. If it is reasonably close, it is warm, and the performer indicates the fact by a "come-on" gesture, bring his hands up toward his face and waving them toward his face. If the guess is very close, the performer makes this gesture very vigorously.

To tell a player to make the word he has guessed shorter, the performer holds his hands apart in front of him and then brings them together, palms facing. This is used when a player guesses such a word as *children* and the word wanted is *child*.

If a word guessed should be made longer, or changed from singular to plural, the performer indicates this by holding his hands together, palms touching, and then spreads them apart. (*hat* to *hats*, *book* to *bookcase*, etc.)

To indicate an unimportant word, connective, or syllable, the performer holds out his right hand and then drops it downward, past his right side. That means he will not act it. When the rest of the charade has been guessed, the unimportant word or syllable will become obvious.

In addition to these conventional gestures, any gesture that is self-explanatory is permissible. For instance, holding the hands, fingers extended and palms together, as if at prayer, means *the Bible, church, religious, prayer*, etc.; holding a hand high over the head means tall, and holding the hand close to the floor means *small, short, tiny*, etc.; and pointing a finger at yourself means *me, mine*, etc.

It must always be remembered that during The Game every gesture of the performer must be acknowledged vocally by his teammates; and the faster The Game is played, the more exciting and hilarious it becomes.

54. Word Charades

Many people still enjoy playing the old-fashioned Word Charade, especially when they are with a group that is not familiar with the complicated rules and conventions of The Game. Word Charades have certain advantages over The Game in addition to being less complicated. Instead of having only one person act the charade, a group cooperate in the performance. This puts no one person "on the spot." It is not every one who likes to play solo before an assemblage. Being one of a group gives the individual greater self-confidence and helps him overcome his inhibitions. Also in playing Word Charades costumes and properties are permitted and add to the gaiety of a performance.

To play Word Charades, divide your guests into teams. The first team retires to another room, chooses a word which they are to dramatize, and plan the performance to be given. Then the captain returns to the room and announces how many syllables there are in the word his team has chosen and in what order the syllables are to be dramatized. Various members of the team come into the room in turn and act, with or without dialogue, in such a manner as to give a clue to the sound of the syllables they are dramatizing. Each syllable is dramatized individually and finally the whole word is acted out. The rest of the guests watch the performances and try to guess each syllable as it is acted. The first one to guess the whole word deserves a prize or a high point score.

After the first team has completed its performance. The second team retires, chooses another word, and performs its dramatization.

The charades may be in the form of undersized playlets, each of which tells a story, broken into scenes which dramatize the syllables of the words to be guessed. Here is an example of such a charade.

The word chosen is CONSTITUTION (con-sti-tu-tion). The captain announces: "We shall act a word of four syllables. The syllables will be acted in their right order, and then the whole word will be acted. We shall now act the first syllable." The following is a synopsis of the charade:

FIRST SYLLABLE (Con-)

Two persons enter. One, the Pilot, stands as if on the bridge of a ship, looking intently out to sea. The other, the Helmsman, stands behind him and acts as if he were at the wheel, steering the ship. The Pilot gives the Helmsman his steering directions, all the time rubbing one of his eyes with his hand. Finally the Pilot cannot stand his discomfort longer. He picks up the ship's telephone and calls for a relief. The relief enters and the Pilot, pointing to his eye, says he must go to the sick bay immediately. He says to the relief, "Take over and direct the steering of the ship." The Pilot exits and the relief, taking his place, begins giving directions to the Helmsman. End of Scene I. (*Con* means to direct the steering of.)

SECOND SYLLABLE (sti-)

This scene is supposed to take place in the sick bay of the ship. A Doctor is examining a patient. He prescribes for him and dismisses him. The Pilot (of the previous scene) enters, and tells the Doctor about his eye trouble. The Doctor examines the eye and says it has a boil on the lid. He prescribes for it and dismisses the Pilot. End of Scene II. (A small boil on the eyelid is a sty.)

THIRD SYLLABLE (tu-)

The scene is the same as in Scene II. The Doctor is examining another patient. He prescribes for him and dismisses him. The Pilot enters in a great state of agitation, with his hand over his other eye. He explains how the eye hurts and the Doctor examines it, and tells him it is another boil. "What," exclaims the Pilot, "in both eyes?" "Yes, sir," says the Doctor. "You certainly have a pair of beauties. Do the same thing for th second as I told you to do for the first." End of Scene III.

FOURTH SYLLABLE (tion)

This scene is supposed to take place in the officers' ward room of the ship. The officers and their wives are having a party. Everyone is enjoying himself. The Pilot enters. His eyelids are very red (lipstick can make them so). He bows politely and tries to get attention, but no one will have anything to do with him. He is shunned by all. End of Scene IV.

THE WHOLE WORD (Constitution)

We are back in the sick bay again. The Pilot enters. He is very angry and upset. The Doctor asks him what is the matter. He explains to the Doctor how he had to call for a relief, because of his eye; how he came to the Doctor for treatment, and went back on duty; how the very next day he had to call for a relief, because of the other eye, and his fellow officers made nasty remarks about it; and how he went to the officers' party and was cold-shouldered by everyone. What's the matter with him, he wants to know. The Doctor feels his biceps, and tells him to dance a jig and then listens to his heart. The Doctor shakes his head and says, "No good. Your physique is shot to pieces. Your lungs wheeze; your heart thumps; your stomach is out of order; you have flat feet and housemaid's elbow, and you are generally run-down." "What shall I do?" asks the Pilot. The Doctor says, "Do what I tell you to, and perhaps we can get you back to health again." End of Scene v.

Charades need not be in the form of a play. Each syllable can be acted in pantomime as a unit in itself, and the pantomime for one syllable need have no relation to the pantomime for any of the other syllables. Here is an example of this kind of a charade.

The word chosen for this charade is ANTIAIRCRAFT (ant-ti-air-craft).

FIRST SYLLABLE (Ant-)

The entire team huddles together, on all fours, in a corner of the room (the ant hill), a pretty girl in the center of the group, with, if such is available, a paper crown on her head to indicate that she is the queen. One member of the team crawls away from the group, and, going this way and that way, like an ant, he comes upon some food (a crumpled piece of paper). He drags the food back to the ant hill. End of Scene I.

SECOND SYLLABLE (ti-)

The members of the team act as if they were at a tea party. Some sit and some walk around chatting with each other. One pours the tea, another passes the cups, etc. End of Scene II.

THIRD SYLLABLE (air-)

Several members of the team sit in chairs and act as if they were suffocating. One of them finally obtains an electric fan, plugs it in and turns it on. The others, with great relief, draw deep breaths. End of Scene III.

FOURTH SYLLABLE (craft)

Some of the team occupy themselves with different crafts. The girls might sew or knit or paint. The men might carve soap, whittle, or repair furniture. End of Scene IV.

127

The team together acts as if the members were manning an antiaircraft battery, shooting upwards at airplanes. End of charade.

For best results with charades, the guests at a party where charades are to be part of the activity program should be told early during the party that charades will be given. The teams should be chosen at that time and captains appointed. The captains may then hold a meeting of their teams to select several words for the charades and plan the action. This will give the captains an opportunity to inform the hostess as to what costumes and properties are needed for the charades and give the hostess time to collect as many of the desired items as are available in her house. Charades are an excellent pastime with which to conclude the activity program of a party.

55. Idiosyncracies

This is another amusement which will give your guests a chance to display their histrionic abilities. One person is sent out of the room, while the others select an adverb which is descriptive of a person's manner, characteristic, or idiosyncrasy, such as *winsomely, snobbishly, stutteringly, enthusiastically*, etc. When the adverb has been decided upon, the person sent from the room is recalled. He is told to ask various persons in the room any questions he wishes and that the answers will be given in the manner of which the adverb chosen is descriptive. He is then to guess what the adverb is.

Suppose the adverb chosen is *comically*. The first person to be questioned might put this thumbs in his ears and wiggle his fingers while he answers. Another might alter his voice and try to imitate Arthur Godfrey, Jackie Gleason, or Gracie Allen. Another might answer with a wisecrack.

An interesting variation of this game is to have a person choose an adverb for himself and keep it to himself.

The other members of the party then, each in turn, command the player to perform some act in the manner of the adverb. The first person to guess what the adverb is then chooses for himself an adverb and follows the commands of the other players.

Such commands as the following may be given: Read from a book in the manner of the adverb. Lie on the sofa in the manner of the adverb. Kiss your partner in the manner of the adverb. Walk across the room in the manner of the adverb. Etc., etc.

56. Photoplay Fun

Here is a humdinger for a small party of 5 to 7 intelligent and imaginative couples.

Each of the ladies is supplied with a pencil, paper, and a male collaborator. Each lady then, with the aid of her collaborator, writes the first scene of a photoplay scenario, either a slapstick farce or hair-raising thriller. The more absurd and outlandish the story, the more fun there will be later. After a time limit of four or five minutes has expired, each of the male collaborators leaves his first lady and teams up with a second lady, and collaborates with her on the second scene of her scenario. After another period of five minutes, he goes to a third lady and helps her with the creation of the third scene of her scenario. This continues until every lady has written one scene with every man. There will then be as many complete scenarios as there are couples and each scenario will have as many scenes as there are male collaborators.

Now the scenarios are read aloud and a vote is taken as to which is the most entertaining. The lady author of the winning scenario is then called upon to present her masterpiece with the aid of any of the guests she may select. The scenario may be acted in the manner of the old days of the silent screen, with the captions being read aloud by a narrator and with a nimble-fingered ivory tickler strumming out appropriate tunes on a piano.

57. Proposals

This hazardous competition will not only afford the spectator great amusement, but it may also prove to be the turning point, for better or worse, in the lives of some of those who participate. Maybe it should be reserved solely for gatherings of bachelors and maidens.

Partners are chosen, either by one of the several methods suggested elsewhere in this book, or by other means; and each couple is then led in turn to a sofa placed in full view of the assemblage. The lady is instructed to be seated, and the gentleman is told to act out a convincing proposal. Prizes are awarded to the couple judged by the guests to have given the most entertaining or the most convincing performance. Of course, the ladies are under no obligation to accept the proposals.

58. Proverbial Histrionics

Most actors will agree that the most difficult performance with which they have to cope is pantomime, action without words. In pantomime, actions and facial expressions must speak for themselves. Proverbial Histrionics offers your guests a rare opportunity of practicing the art of the pantomimist.

Divide the company into two teams. Explain that each player on both teams is to write on a piece of paper a proverb, maxim, or quotation and then fold the piece of paper. The folded pieces of paper are then exchanged between members of the two teams, so that every member of Team A has a quotation written by a member of Team B, and every member of Team B has a quotation written by a member of Team A. It is strictly illegal for a player to reveal to another member of his team what quotation he has received until he has dramatized it.

After the quotations have been exchanged, the first player of Team A is requested to arise and, for the benefit of his own teammates, act out, in pantomime, the quotation given to him. His teammates must guess from his performance the words of his quotation. If they succeed, the member of his team who first guesses the quotation scores 5 points, and the first player on Team B then arises and, for the benefit of his teammates, acts out the quotation given to him, and the members of his team try to guess it. After all of the players, alternating in turn, have acted their quotations, the team holding the greatest number of points among all of its members, wins.

No performer is permitted to re-enact his quotation more than once, or twice at the most; and his teammates must make a decision within a reasonable time, two or three minutes. If the quotation has not been guessed within the time limit, each player on the opposing team scores one point. Performers are permitted to use "props," if what they want can easily and quickly be provided by the hostess.

Some appropriate quotations for this pastime are the following.

> A stitch in time saves nine.
> When angry count ten before you speak.
> One good turn deserves another.
> A bad workman quarrels with his tools.
> Hit the nail on the head.
> Look before you leap.
> Rob Peter and pay Paul
> Strike the iron while it is hot.
> There's a time for all things.
> Ring out the old, ring in the new.

59. Shadow Play

Shadow play is an ancient and honorable sport that must date back beyond the dark ages to the day when man first became conscious of his shadow cast by the sun. The possibilities of employing your shadow for entertainment are limited only by the bounds of your own originality and imagination.

For indoor shadow play you will need a sheet and a strong electric lamp, preferably with a reflector. Hang the sheet between two rooms where there is an archway or folding doors. In one room place the lamp on a table six or seven feet from the sheet. This room is the stage. In the other room, the auditorium, arrange a sufficient number of chairs, facing the sheet, to accommodate the audience.

Divide your guests into two teams, and send the first team to the stage, while the second team occupies the seats in the auditorium.

Back stage you have provided such "props" and costumes as are available in your house: old hats, coats, masks, false whiskers, canes, etc. You tell the first team to dress themselves up in any way they have a mind to. Give them some newspapers with which they can make whatever accessories they may need. Explain to them that they, one at a time, are to step between the light and the sheet and act in some outlandish manner, dance a jig, do setting-up exercises, stand on their heads, crawl on all fours, anything; but always keep side-faced to the sheet, and move from right to left. Their shadows in profile, must always be on the sheet. Of course the closer they perform to the sheet, the more natural they will appear, and the nearer they are to the light, the more grotesque their shadows will be.

After all this has been explained to the team members and they have been allowed ten or fifteen minutes in which to disguise themselves, you turn out the lights in the auditorium and the leader of the first team turns out all the lights back stage, excepting the lamp on the table which is reflected towards the sheet. Then each member of the first team appears in turn on the sheet, in shadow, and the members of the second team try to guess the identity of each shadow. Of course there is no speaking.

A point is scored for the second team every time it identifies one of the players of the first team. But the identification must be made within two minutes after the close of an individual's performance. After the last member of the first team has performed and all the guesses of the second team have been registered, the first and second teams exchange places, and the first team tries to identify the members of the second team as they appear in shadows. The team making the greatest number of points wins.

60. Shadow Show

Another way of having fun with Shadow Play is to have the teams act charades in shadow only, no words to be spoken. When acting shadow charades, the players act their parts close to the sheet, so that the audience can see more clearly just what they are doing.

Shadow charades require rather careful planning, so the teams, especially their captains, should be informed early what is to be expected of them. They may then plan their charades to better advantage than otherwise.

If you have shadow charades, divide your group into teams of not more than five or six members each. While one team acts the shadow charade, the other teams sit in the audience and guess what word is being dramatized.

5. Oral Games

61. The Adjective Game

IF A PARTY that has shown signs of turning serious and sticky can not have life and laughter injected in it by this old standby, there is nothing to be done but call the whole thing off, evict the guests, and close up the house.

Before the party begins write a news report, of about 600 words, describing what is expected to take place, just as if it had already happened. The report should mention the names of all the persons expected to be present and also others known to all the guests. It should describe the entertainment provided and tell what various guests wore, said, and did. However, in writing the report, adjectives should be omitted and in front of every noun a space is left blank.

When the time comes to introduce the game, the hostess asks each guest in turn to supply an adjective of a particularly unpleasant, approbrious, or invective nature, such as monstrous, vulgar, misshapen, tight-fisted, gawky, oafish, slovenly, priggish, etc. As the adjectives are suggested, the hostess writes them in the blank spaces in the news report she has previously prepared. When all of the blanks have been filled in, she announces that her guests, unknown to them, have written a charming report of the evening's gaieties, and then proceeds to read the report aloud, adjectives and all.

62. Avoid 'Em

Your guests will have to mind their P's and Q's, as well as the *m*'s, *t*'s and other letters of the alphabet when they play this game. It sounds simple but it isn't.

The game begins by the leader saying, "I don't like *m*," and then asking each player in turn a question. Each question must be answered sensibly without employing a word which contains the letter *m*. If the player answers incorrectly, he has a point charged against him.

The leader might ask the first person, "What day follows Sunday?" and the answer could be, "The day before Tuesday." It could not be "Monday" because that word contains an *m*. His next question might be, "What makes an automobile go?" The answer could be gasoline (or a gasoline engine). It could not be "A motor."

If the questioning goes completely around the group without any one making a mistake, a new leader takes up the questioning, choosing a new letter to be avoided. He would say, "I don't like *t* (or whatever letter it is he doesn't want)."

This game can be continued until every guest has had a chance to serve as leader. Then the scores are added and the player with the lowest score wins.

It is permissible for the leader to use in his questioning words which contain the disliked letter, but no other player may use such words in his answer.

63. Boob

Silly games are often more fun for a crowd than intelligent, serious games. Just because a game sounds silly, don't pass it by without giving it a trial. Some evening when the boss, or some other industrial big shots, have to be entertained try this silly-sounding game. Silly-sounding though it is, it is more fun than you may believe at first hearing, and not so easy as it sounds.

The object of the game is for your guests to salute each other in the well-known tradition of big business, by using initials only; but the catch is that the initials used are not those of the name of the player saluted, but the first letters of a four- or six-letter word. The players saluted must acknowledge the salute by using the last letters required to complete a word.

If that isn't clear, you will get the idea from these examples.

Mr. Smith begins the game by saying to Mr. Jones, "Hi, B. O." Mr. Jones replies, "Howdy, O. B." thereby completing the word Boob. Mr. Jones then salutes Mr. Pink, saying, "Hello, P. U. T." and Mr. Pink replies,

"How you doing, R. I. D." completing the word Putrid. Get the idea?

The saluter must have a bona-fide word in mind and is subject to challenge. If when challenged he is unable to name an acceptable English word, he must pay a fine, or have a point charged against him, or be disqualified. If the saluted player is unable to complete a word in ten seconds, he likewise must pay a fine, have a point charged against him, or be disqualified.

These lists of four- and six-letter words will give you an inkling of the possibilities of this game.

AP-EX	APO-LLO
BU-NK	BAD-GER
CA-RD	BIG-WIG
CH-AP	BOB-CAT
DA-FF	CAC-TUS
FI-RE	CHE-RUB
FL-IP	DAZ-ZLE
HO-BO	FLO-WER
HE-EL	HAR-LOT
LO-VE	MAR-VEL
MA-TE	PRE-TTY
PL-UG	STU-PID
UG-LY	VUL-GAR

64. Buzz

Your guests, seated in a circle, count off. The player who begins says 1, the player next to him says 2, the third player says 3, and so on around the circle, each player in turn calling out the next highest number, excepting when a 7 or any multiple of 7 comes up, and that is where the fun comes in. No player may say 7 or a multiple of 7; but instead must say, "buzz." So the counting would be like this: 1, 2, 3, 4, 5, 6, buzz, 8, 9, 10, 11, 12, 13, buzz, 15, 16, one buzz, 18, 19, 20, buzz, 22, 23, 24, 25, 26, two buzz, buzz, 29, 30, 31, 32, 33, 34, buzz, 36, three buzz, etc. The counting should be as rapid as possible, and anyone who fails to buzz at the right time is eliminated from the game, or has a point charged against him. The survivor, the one who has no points against him, wins.

65. Confabulation

Confabulation is a highly entertaining pastime for good conversationalists, public speakers, lawyers, and wind bags. Shy, sensitive bivalves and those who are known never to say much more than "Yes" or "No" or "I think so" should not be asked to participate excepting as innocent bystanders.

A couple is sent out of the room and those left behind make up two sentences, one for the man and one for the girl. The two sentences should be as ridiculous as possible and totally different in subject matter. The couple is called back into the room and seated beside each other in front of the guests. Each is then given his sentence, written on a piece of paper, and is told to memorize his sentence.

Now the fun begins. The couple is directed to carry on a conversation with each other and each is to endeavor to incorporate in the conversation the sentence given to him without revealing to the opponent that that was the particular sentence which was required. If the opponent thinks that a certain sentence is the one required, he or she says right away, "That is what you were told to say." If he or she is right, he or she is the victor. If mistaken, the conversation continues. If one succeeds in using the required sentence without being challenged, that one wins.

Supposing the man is given this sentence: *Roosters skid when they walk on ice;* and the girl is given this one: *Soon every house will have an airplane hangar on its roof.* Then the conversation might be something like this.

Man: Do you enjoy skating?
Girl: Yes indeed on big lakes, but we live a long way from a big lake and the transportation is too slow. I wish we had an airplane. Do you do much flying?

Man: No, I keep close to the ground. I like skating
   better than flying. We flood our garden in the winter
   and skate on that when it freezes. We have great fun.
Girl: Oh, flying is much more fun. I am just waiting
   for the day when I can have my own plane. You
   know, soon every house will have an airplane hanger
   on its roof.
Man: That is what you were told to say.

SOME OTHER SENTENCES:

For the Man: It is wise not to step on banana peels.
For the Girl: Turtles cannot climb a ladder.
For the Man: It is not good manners to smoke in church.
For the Girl: Flea bites have nothing to do with phlebitis.

66. District Attorney

Few games have as great possibilities as this for pro-
ducing spine-chills, gooseflesh, and sheer excitement
among the players. It can be played by any group of
half a dozen or more persons with agile imaginations,
among whom is one person with a good memory.

It is very simply explained. The person with the good
memory is designated District Attorney. One other is
secretly chosen to announce, at an appointed time, the
discovery of the corpse of a murdered individual.

At the appointed moment, the discoverer of the corpse
rushes into the room where the players are assembled,
and describes the gruesome imaginary details of finding
in the house or very nearby the mutilated corpse of some
one who is known to all the players, but who is not
present. In describing what he pretends took place, he
implicates one of the other players, casting upon him
the shadow of suspicion of murder.

The District Attorney then takes over, and commences
an investigation, ordering all of the players to remain in
the room, and explaining to them that everything that is
said in answer to his questions must be held to be true
and cannot afterward be contradicted by anyone. He
then proceeds to question the discoverer of the corpse
and everyone who is thereafter implicated in the testi-

mony, in an effort to ascertain who committed the crime. Each person questioned tries in his answers to disassociate himself from the murder and at the same time tries to implicate one of the other players.

It is clearly apparent whither such a proceeding will lead. If the game is played intelligently and seriously, sooner or later one of the players will become so overwhelmed with circumstantial evidence that the murder can be pinned on to him beyond reasonable doubt.

The rules governing this game are few. Everything said by a witness in answer to the District Attorney's questions is held to be true and cannot thereafter be contradicted by anyone. There cannot be any eyewitness to the crime. The District Attorney may ask any questions he desires and must question everyone implicated by the testimony, including the discoverer of the corpse. Only the District Attorney is permitted to ask questions, although others may suggest questions to him.

Any one is capable of serving as District Attorney who has a sufficiently good memory to prevent conflicting or contradictory testimony from entering the game. All such testimony must be instantly ruled out. It must be emphasized that everything said during the questioning must be accepted as fact and cannot be changed or contradicted. It is the responsibility of the District Attorney to see that such does not happen.

67. Essentially Different

Psychological tests have become very popular as party pastimes. As a matter of fact most of the brain-teaser games in this book are adaptations of tests developed by psychologists for measuring or analyzing the intelligence of individuals. The object of this test is to determine an individual's ability to quickly distinguish things of one class from things of another class. This is done by calling out four words, three of which are in the same category and one of which is in a different category. For example, the four words could be *comma, colon, hyphen, period. Comma, colon,* and *period* are punctuation marks and are in one category, but *hyphen* is not a punctuation mark and therefore is in a different category, and is disassociated from the other three words.

In playing this as a game, the leader calls four words out to the first player, who is allowed exactly ten seconds in which to name the disassociated word. If the player succeeds, he scores one point. If he fails, he scores nothing. The second player is then given four other words, then the third, and so on around the group.

Any one can make up his own list of words. The following list is intended to serve as a guide.

1. Oldsmobile, Buick, Sedan, Dodge
2. Spar, Prow, Sheet, Halyard
3. Canary, parakeet, bird, robin
4. See, Feel, Hear, Say
5. Geometry, Philosophy, Psychology, Sociology
6. Comma, Colon, Hyphen, Period
7. Alcohol, Gin, Whiskey, Rum
8. Harp, Violin, Drum, Orchestra
9. Crayon, Chalk, Writing, Paper
10. Dickens, Freud, Tarkington, Hemingway
11. Booth, Barrymore, Truman, Mansfield
12. Rug, Room, Chair, Table
13. Orchard, Woods, Tree, Forest
14. Amorous, Affectionate, Sweetheart, Loving
15. Love, Mean, Hate, Fear
16. Beans, Pears, Onions, Carrots
17. One, Three, Six, Five
18. United States, England, Asia, Russia
19. Boston, Atlanta, Oregon, Omaha
20. Chops, Calf, Cutlets, Steak
21. Captain, Major, Colonel, General Staff
22. Fire, Wood, Coke, Coal
23. Boil, Bake, Cook, Fry
24. Home Plate, Pitcher, First Base, Foul Line
25. Endeavor, Start, Attempt, Strive

68. First Word Rhyming

Be sure of your company before suggesting this game, because it is one of those games, which, if played with sharp-witted persons, will be a laugh-provoking business; but if played by those who are of a more or less sensitive and retiring nature and who do not think quickly on their feet, may be a dud and the cause of much embarrassment. In other words, it is a good game with the right crowd.

Here is how it is done. It is very easily explained. Some one asks some one else a question. Let's say, "Where is my hat?" Now here is the catch. The person asked the question must *begin* his answer with a word that rhymes with the *last* word in the question. From then on each player in turn must make a statement, the first word of which rhymes with the last word of the statement made by the preceding player.

This is how it might go.

> *1st Player:* Where is my hat?
> *2nd Player:* That I cannot say.
> *3rd Player:* Day is light; night is dark
> *4th Player:* Hark the herald angels sing.
> *5th Player:* Ring out the old; ring in the new.
> *6th Player:* Chew well what you eat.
> *7th Player:* Beat the baby when he sneezes.

The player who fails to respond quickly or who gives an incorrect rhyme, or whose statement does not make sense is either dropped from the game or has a point charged against his score.

69. Globe Circling

A large wall map of the world and a box of thumb tacks are required for this game, which, if played at a quick pace, can be very exciting.

Divide the players into two teams and have each team select a leader, who is provided with a supply of thumb tacks. The teams are told that they are to race around the world, each starting from the same city, but moving in opposite directions, one going east and the other west. A city is then chosen for the starting point. The leader of Team A which is to travel West then calls to the first player on his team the name of the state in which the starting point is, and the player must instantly name the capital of that state. If he names it correctly, the leader pins one of his thumb tacks in the center of the state on

141

the map. If the player is wrong, the second player tries to name the capital of that state. If he is wrong, the third player guesses, etc. Meanwhile the leader of Team B, which is traveling East, calls to the first player of his team the name of the next country nearest the starting point, and that player must instantly name the capital of the country. The two teams proceed as quickly as possible in this manner around the world, pinning their thumb tacks on the map as rapidly as their teammates name the capitals called for. The first team to return to the state from which it started is the winner.

This game can be played in many different ways. The teams may race only across the United States, one team starting from the east coat and the other from the west coast, or they might race from Canada to the Argentine, one starting from Montreal and the other from Blanca. In any case the teams must always pass through the next nearest state or country in as direct a line as possible.

70. It Isn't Another

Here is a tricky variation of Twenty Questions. The person chosen to act as questioner leaves the room while the other guests agree upon the name of a person or place which the questioner will be expected to identify. The questioner is called back into the room, and he asks each player in turn a question which can be answered either "Yes" or "No." Now here is where the game differs from Twenty Questions. Each player questioned must include in his answer a name that might have been the name chosen, but is not. In his answer he uses the expression, "Yes, but it is not so-and-so," or "No, it is not so-and-so"; and the names he uses must begin with the same letter with which the name agreed upon begins.

If the name agreed upon were Boston, here is how the questioning and answering might go:

Questioner: Is it a man?
1st Player: No, it is not Beethoven.
Questioner: Is it a woman?
2nd Player: No, it is not Bernhardt.

Questioner: Is it a country?
3rd Player: No, it is not Brazil.
Questioner: Is it a city?
4th Player: Yes, but it is not Bayreuth.
Questioner: Is it in the United States?
5th Player: Yes, but it is not Binghamton.
Questioner: Is it in the state of New York?
6th Player: No, it is not Brewster. Etc., etc.

Players who fail to answer correctly have a point charged against them. Likewise, if the questioner, after a reasonable number of questions (not more than 20), fails to guess the name agreed on, a point is charged against him. After all the players have had a go at being the questioner, the player with the fewest number of points charged against him is the winner. A new questioner should be chosen every time a new name is selected for guessing.

71. The Movie-Goer

Here is a quiz game that is different. The leader begins the game by saying, "I am going to the movies tomorrow and will see so-and-so in such-and-such picture (naming the star and a well-known picture)." Then the leader asks each person in turn a question about the star or the picture—Is the star a blond? Is the picture a comedy? Who plays opposite the star? When was the picture released? Etc., etc.

Each person who answers accurately is given a piece of stage money, or a chip. If a person fails to answer a question, or answers incorrectly, the same question is asked of the next person. When the leader has asked every player one question, a new leader takes his place and announces the name of a new star and the title of a new picture as the subjects of his questions. After every one has had a chance of being the leader, the game is stopped, and the person holding the most money or the greatest number of chips is declared the moving picture expert.

To vary the game, the leader may be a traveler, who will ask questions about a city he is to visit; or he may

be a book reader, who seeks information about a book
he is going to read and about its author. The subject
can be adapted to the interests of your guests. If your
guests are sports lovers, the leader might start by saying, "I am going to see the Dodgers-Giants game"; and
then ask such questions as, Who is the manager of the
Dodgers? Who is the heaviest hitter on the Giants'
team? In what place in the league did the Dodgers end
up last year? How many World Series championships
have the Giants won?

72. Numbers

A good game for the history minded is Numbers. The
first player calls out a number. The player on his right
must immediately say what he associates with that number. If he fails, a point is scored against him, and the
player on his right answers, if he can; and so on around
the group. Each person answering correctly calls out a
new number. The person who calls the number may be
challenged, and if he is unable to give a name, event,
situation, or phrase associated with his number, a point
is scored against him.

The game would go something like this:

1st Player: 7
2nd Player: Come eleven
2nd Player: 16
3rd Player: Sweet 16
3rd Player: 1914
4th Player: Beginning of World War I
4th Player: 25
5th Player: Christmas Day

73. Opposites

For this game the players are divided into two groups,
or teams, which are seated opposite each other in two
facing rows of chairs about four or five feet apart. The
leader, or It, walks back and forth between the two
groups and suddenly points at one of the players and
says a word, speaks a sentence, or asks a question. Now

here is the gag. The person spoken to must remain absolutely silent, but the person sitting directly opposite to the one addressed must instantly answer in the opposite.

This is how it works. It suddenly points at Jimmy Valentine and says, "Black." Jimmy keeps mum, but Sarah Bernhardt, who is sitting directly opposite Jimmy, immediately shouts, "White." It then points at Toots Murphy and says, "You are beautiful." Toots remains silent, but Henry Clay, opposite her, pipes up with, "You are ugly." It might then point at Henry Beecher, and ask, "Is your wife clever?" Hank's opposite would say, "No, my husband is stupid." And so it goes.

If the person pointed at should speak, he or she becomes It. If the opposite person fails to speak up in a few seconds, or if he gives an inappropriate answer, he becomes It. Also, if anyone speaks out of turn, he or she becomes It.

The person who is It should pass rapidly from one to another, first challenging a member of one group and then wheeling around quickly and challenging some one in the opposite group.

For scoring purposes, one point should be chalked up against each person who becomes It and for each member of the opposite team.

74. Spell of Cities

This entertaining game is played by any number of players, one of whom begins by naming a city and then spelling it. If he spells it correctly, the person on his left must then name and correctly spell another city, the name of which must begin with the last letter of the name of the city spelled by the preceding player.

If the first person names and correctly spells Philadelphia, the second player might name and spell Athens, and the third could name and spell Santiago. Three misses disqualifies the player against whom they are scored. The last one remaining in the game, of course, wins; and is entitled to a prize, or 10 points to be added to his accumulated score for the occasion.

If there are more than 8 or 9 persons present, it is best to divide them into two teams for this game. In this case, the first person on one team begins and is followed by the first person on the other team, then the second person on the first team, then the second person on the second team, etc. Misses are counted as one point each against the team whose member makes the error. The team with the lowest number of points when the game is halted wins.

75. Suggestions

Although this game can be played with enjoyment anywhere at any time, it is just right for a picnic group sitting around an open fire. It begins by one person naming any object. He might say, "Shovel." The person on his right then must name another article which the first article suggests to him. He might say, "Coal." The third person, to the right, then names something suggested by coal. He might say, "Bin." The next player might say, "Cellar"; the fifth player, "House." So it goes several times around the circle. Then comes the hard part. The object is to reverse the order of play, and try to trace back the suggestions.

Let's suppose the game has gone around the circle three times and the players are told to retrace the suggestions. The last person to name an object must immediately name correctly the object named by the preceding player, and the preceding player must then name the object named by the player directly preceding him.

The first half of the game is played from left to right; and the second half, from right to left.

Those who make mistakes either are dropped out or have points scored against them.

76. Teapot

He told Susie not to teapot the teapot of teapots, but to teapot only one teapot, because she was allowed only one teapot. Simple, isn't it? If you can translate that

146

sentence you ought to be good at this game, which requires the players always to substitute the word *teapot* for a chosen word that has more than one meaning, or for several words that are pronounced alike but have different meanings. The first sentence means, *He told Susie not to pare the pair of pears, but to pare only one pear, because she was allowed only one pear.*

Now, here is how the game is played.

One player is dismissed from the room, and the others choose two or more words that are pronounced alike but have different meanings, such as *so, sew,* and *sow; rain, rein, reign;* or *role, roll* (move by turning over and over), *roll* (a small cake of bread). When the words have been chosen the dismissed player returns to the room and asks each person in turn any question he wishes. The person questioned must include in his answer the word *teapot* in the sense of one of the words chosen, and the questioner must try to guess what word *teapot* stands for.

For example, if the words chosen are *bare, bear* (to hold up), and *bear* (the animal), the questions and answers might be something like this:

> *Questioner:* What news have you heard lately?
> *1st Player:* A good story about a teapot.
> *Questioner:* What happened in the story?
> *2nd Player:* The teapot got away.
> *Questioner:* Who tried to get it?
> *3rd Player:* The teapot man who had been in swimming in the river.
> *Questioner:* What did the man do?
> *4th Player:* He ran to his tent, grabbed his gun, took a shot at the teapot and teapotly missed him.

If at this point the questioner guesses the words bear and bare(ly), the 4th Player becomes the questioner and leaves the room, while the others choose another group of words pronounced alike but having different meanings. If the questioner does not guess the words correctly, he continues to ask questions. Whoever answers the last question before the questioner guesses the chosen words becomes the next questioner.

147

Here are some other words that can be used for the game:

sun, son
bank (a ridge), bank (financial institution), bank (tier)
bar (crowbar), bar (sand), bar (legal profession), bar (counter)
wring, ring (a bell), ring (for the finger)
boar, bore (drill), bore (a stupid)
tip (end or top), tip (fee), tip (overturn)
through (from end to end), through (finished), threw (hurled)

77. Touring with the Alphabet

A sharp ear and a good memory are needed for touring with the alphabet. The players sit around a circle, and the one who starts the game says, "I am going on a journey and will take with me an atlas." The player on his left must repeat, word for word, what the first player has said and add the name of something the spelling of which begins with the letter B. He might say, "I am going on a journey and will take with me an atlas and baggage." The next player on the left repeats this, word for word, and adds something spelled with C. He might say, "I am going on a journey and will take with me an atlas and baggage and a coat." The fourth player repeats everything the third player has said and adds something beginning with a D. And so on through the alphabet. Any one who fails to repeat accurately what the previous player has said, or who cannot add something spelled with the required letter, has a point charged against him and the player on his left continues the game, if he can. It is not often that the entire alphabet is completed in this game, but it is fun to see how far a group can go.

A variation of this game is for the first player to say, "I am going on a tour and will visit Athens." The other players must then, each in turn, add the name of another city in alphabetical order.

78. Twenty Questions

If not the oldest of the quiz games, Twenty Questions is probably the best known. Its variations are almost unlimited. One way to play it is to send a player from the room while the others agree upon some thing animate or inanimate, which the player sent from the room must identify upon his return by asking each player in turn a question which can be answered "yes" or "no." If he can identify the thing agreed upon within the limits of twenty questions, he scores as many points as the difference between the number of questions he asked before he identified the thing and 21. For example, if he guessed the identity of the thing after asking 15 questions, he would score 6 points; if he guessed the identity after asking 20 questions, he would score 1 point. No player is allowed more than 20 questions, so if the player fails to identify the thing chosen within 20 questions, he cannot score. The person having the largest number of points at the end of the game wins.

Another way to play the game is for one player to announce, "I am thinking of something," and the other players, each in turn, ask him a question that can be answered "yes" or "no." The first person in the group to guess what thing the leader is thinking of then becomes the leader. The person who most frequently guesses correctly is the expert guesser.

However the game is played, the questions must be answered either "yes" or "no." No further information is to be given.

79. Vocabulary Speed

This amusing game can be played orally or with pencil and paper. It is very simple, but really a lot of fun. If it is played orally, the leader assigns a letter of the alphabet to each player in turn and the player sees how many good English words beginning with that letter he can name in a period of 60 seconds.

If the game is played with pencil and paper, the leader assigns the same letter to all the players and simultaneously they all write the words. Each player scores one point for every word he has written within the one minute time limit. The player with the highest score at the end of the game wins.

Each time the game is played, a new letter is assigned but never the letters X and Z.

80. Who Am I?

To play this laugh-provoking game you send one player from the room and have those remaining choose some character they wish the one sent from the room to represent. The character chosen may be taken from history or literature, or may be any living person who is wellknown to all who are participating in the game. When a character has been decided upon, the excluded player is called back into the room and is told to find out who he is by asking each of the other players in turn the single question, "Who am I?" Each person to whom this question is addressed must, in reply, give some clue to the identity of the character the questioner is supposed to represent.

Suppose Winston Churchill is the character chosen. The first person asked, "Who am I?" might reply, You have traveled extensively. The second person could say, You are a soldier. The third person could reply, You are a writer. The fourth, You are married. The fifth, You are a navy man. And so the questioning and answering might proceed, each player trying to avoid mentioning in his answers the attributes or activities for which the character is best known.

When the questioner finally guesses his identity, the person who answered last and provided the missing clue takes the place of the questioner and leaves the room while a new character is selected for him to represent. And the game goes on.

81. Ghosts

This very popular game is known by a variety of names—Chain Spelling, Monkey, etc. Call it what you want, it is always a success. It is a particularly good game to play at the dinner table, or when sitting around the camp or picnic fire.

One person starts the fun by thinking of a word of three or more letters and, without saying what the word is, announces the first letter with which it is spelled. The person on his left then thinks of a word of three or more letters which begins with the letter announced by the first player and says what the second letter is. Each person in turn then adds another letter, always having in mind a correct English word that the combination of letters announced will help to spell. The object of the game is to avoid calling a letter that will complete a word. When some one adds the final letter forming a word, a miss is scored against him. Three misses make him a ghost and he must be completely ignored by everyone not a ghost. He may talk to any one he wishes and try to inveigle others into speaking to him; but whoever is foolish enough to converse with a ghost, himself becomes one. When all but one have become ghosts the game ends and the remaining human is declared the winner.

The game might proceed in this manner. The first player thinks of the word *money* and calls the letter M. The next player on his left thinks of the word *manner* and adds to the M an A. The third player thinks of *magic* and adds to the MA a G. The fourth player thinks of *magnum* and adds to the MAG an N. The fifth player thinks of *magnify* and adds to the MAGN an I. The sixth player also thinks of *magnify* and adds to the MAGNI an F, hoping to catch the person on his left. But the person on his left fools him by thinking of the word *magnifier* and adds to the MAGNIF an I. The eighth player thinks of *magnified* and adds to the combination of letters an E, which forces the ninth player to complete a word by adding an s, r, or d.

Any player may challenge any other player to name the word he has in mind. If his word is not a correct English word or if it cannot be correctly spelled with the combination of letters available, he then has a miss scored against him. If he has a perfectly good word, then the challenger has a miss scored against him.

6. Paper and Pencil Games

82. Building Pictures

THIS IS an excellent competitive game for small teams of three or four players, although it is also good fun when played by individuals, each man for himself.

From magazines, cut out a large and varied assortment of pictures of people and things—trees, houses, cars, furniture, animals, anything that catches your fancy. This you may do before your party, or you may supply each of your guests with a pair of scissors and a magazine, and have them do their own cutting-out, making their own selection of pictures.

All of the cutouts are put in a box or basket and placed on a table in the center of the room. The participating teams can sit on the floor or at card tables, each team at a different table. Each team is supplied with a tube of paste, a sheet of paper or Bristol board, about 10 x 14 inches in size, and a small box of colored crayons.

When all is arranged, the hostess announces a quotation or title, and the players are told to illustrate it, choosing whatever cutouts they want from the available supply and pasting them where they will on the pieces of paper or Bristol board, filling in with the crayons anything that may be required to perfect the picture.

At the end of a specified time, say 25 minutes, the pasted-up pictures are put on exhibition and judged. The team, or individual, whose picture is judged to be most original and amusing wins.

Here are a few appropriate titles for this game:

THE GOOD OLD SUMMER TIME
MAIN STREET
THE SIDEWALKS OF NEW YORK
GONE WITH THE WIND
THE DELUGE
A MIDSUMMER NIGHT'S DREAM
BOY MEETS GIRL
THE GREEN PASTURES

83. Categories

This is one of the most widely employed "brain teasers" and for that reason alone deserves a place in any collection of party pastimes.

Provide each player with a pencil and a sheet of paper. Select some word of four or more letters, preferably one in which no letter of the alphabet appears more than once, such as PASTIME. Tell each player to write the letters of the word on the left side of his sheet of paper, as near the edge as possible, one letter under the other, with generous space between the letters. Then tell him to draw 5 or 6 vertical lines, from top to bottom of his sheet of paper, about an inch apart, and draw horizontal lines across the paper, one under each letter, so that each letter will appear at the left of a series of frames or boxes.

Now ask your guests to suggest categories. Supposing the first guest suggests FLOWERS. Tell each player to head the first column on his sheet of paper with the word FLOWERS. Some one else may then suggest BIRDS, and this word is to head the second column. A third person may suggest VEGETABLES, and this word will go at the head of the third column. A fourth suggestion might be ACTRESSES and that word will be written at the head of the fourth column. A fifth suggestion for the top of the fifth column might be KINGS. The categories may refer to any class of living or inanimate things, such as statesmen, soldiers, fishes, snakes, cities, colleges, etc.

If the word chosen were PASTIME each player's sheet of paper would be lined to look like this:

FLOWERS	BIRDS	VEGETABLES	ACTRESSES	KINGS
P Pansy	Popinjay	Pea		
A Aster				
S Sunflower				
T				
I				
M				
E				

The object of the game is for each player to fill in the empty frames on his sheet of paper with appropriate names of things in the categories chosen and which begin with the letters that are written at the left of the sheet of paper.

If you will look carefully at the illustration you will see how this is done. Under the heading FLOWERS a player must write the name of a flower beginning with P, say *pansy*. Directly under that, in the next frame, he must write the name of a flower beginning with A, it could be *aster*. In the next frame under that he could write *sunflower*. All of the other frames are to be filled in in the same manner, according to the categories named at the top of the columns and the letters appearing at the left of the paper. So, under BIRDS, *popinjay* might be written in the first frame; and under VEGE-TABLES, *pea* could be written in the first frame.

When one player has filled in all of his frames, or after a reasonable time has elapsed, the game is stopped and the achievements of the players are scored. The players call out in turn each word they have used, reading down the columns; and each frame is scored in this manner. If a player has used a word no other player has used, he scores 10 points for that frame, otherwise he scores 1 point for the frame; unless, of course, he has used an incorrect word or has left the frame vacant, in which case he scores zero for the frame. The players add up their scores for all the frames, and the one with the largest number of points wins.

Every time the game is replayed a new word is selected to provide the letters to be written down the left side of the paper and new categories to head the columns.

Instead of providing a word, you may have the players select five or six different letters, a different player selecting each letter.

84. Clothing

The surprise ending to this guessing game never fails to get a laugh.

All of your guests are seated and each is given a pencil

and a sheet of paper. They are then told that a female model will walk around the room, exhibiting a new ensemble, and they are to note carefully what she is wearing. When she leaves the room, they are told that each guest is to write down every item of wearing apparel he or she remembers seeing on the model. The model appears and is "dressed to kill," with everything on she can get on, including hat, gloves, jewelry, etc. The more items she is able to exhibit, the better. She walks around the room for two minutes and then leaves.

The guests are allowed ten minutes in which to write down what the model wore. The lists are then read and checked.

Then comes the surprise. The guests are informed that now a male model will exhibit an ensemble. A man then enters the room, dressed only in bathing trunks, walks once around the room and leaves. Now the guests are given five minutes, not to write down what the man wore, but to write down a complete list of the items of clothing he will wear when he appears again fully dressed. While they are doing this, the male model gets dressed, and when the allotted time has expired, he returns and tells exactly what he has on, naming every item. The guests check their lists.

In the case of both the male's clothing lists and the female's clothing lists, one point is scored for each correct item and one point is deducted for each incorrect item. The guest with the highest score, needless to say, deserves some kind of a reward.

85. Comparisons

In the good old days, the belle of the ball was always *pretty as a picture*, or *fair as a lily*; the crabbed old gentleman was *as cross as two sticks*; the smart little boy was *as bright as a button*; and the embarrassed young suitor turned *red as a beet*.

There are many of these comparative expressions, which are well known to everybody, that can be illustrated by objects. A form of amusement is to arrange on a table a dozen or more plates, on each of which is an object which suggests one of these threadworn sayings, and then have people guess the saying each represents. Each guest is given a pencil and piece of paper; and each plate, of course, is numbered. Each guest writes on his paper the numbers of the plates and the saying illustrated by what is on each plate.

The winner is the person who first guesses all the sayings illustrated, or who after the expiration of a stated time guesses the greatest number of sayings.

Among the objects that may be used for this game are a lily (*as fair as a lily*), a ping-pong bat (*as blind as a bat*), a button (*as bright as a button*), a cut-glass tumbler or wine glass (*as clear as crystal*), a beet (*as red as a beet*), a feather (*as light as a feather*), two sticks crossed (*as cross as two sticks*), the lead from a pencil (*as heavy as lead*), a whistle (*as clean as a whistle*), a gold ring or trinket (*as good as gold*), a brass candle stick, upholstering tack, or curtain ring (*as bold as brass*), a small glass with just a swallow of water in it (*as swift as a swallow*), a doornail (*as dead as a doornail*), a pancake (*as flat as a pancake*), the ace of spades (*as black as the ace of spades*), a handful of mud (*as thick as mud*), etc.

86. Commit to Memory

How keenly do you observe things and how well do you remember what you have seen? This fascinating game is an exercise in seeing and remembering.

Place a dozen different small objects on a tray, cover the tray with a cloth, and place it on a table in the center of the room. Have your guests stand in a circle around the table, so that every one has an unobstructed view of the tray. Now tell your guests that you will expose the contents of the tray for two minutes and they are to remember what they will see on the tray.

Remove the cloth from the tray, and after two minutes replace it over the tray. Now each of your guests is to write down on a slip of paper provided for the purpose the name of every article he remembers having seen on the tray.

While the guests are doing this, take the tray to another room, and add a dozen more articles to the original collection, cover the tray as before, and replace it on the table where it was first viewed.

After allowing the guests ten minutes in which to write their first lists, gather them around the tray again, and let them view the new collection of articles for *three* minutes, and then recover the tray. Now instruct your guests to revise their original lists by adding to them as many articles as they remember having seen at the second viewing.

Allow another ten minutes for writing the second lists. Then remove the cloth from the tray, and have each guest check his list for errors and omissions. The one who has the longest list of correctly named articles wins the game. Or each player may count 1 point for every correctly named article.

The following articles are suitable for this memory test.

Beer-can opener	Rose	Flashlight battery
Colored pencil	Feather	Calling card
Safety-pin	Life saver	Wrist watch
Door key	Elastic band	Toothpick
Penny postcard	Cigarette lighter	Pair of scissors, open
Pocket knife	Paper matches	Curtain ring
Clothespin	Piece of camphor	Snapshot
Paper-clip	Silver teaspoon	Candle

87. Consequences

Almost everybody knows this old favorite, but it is included in this book for the benefit of any one who doesn't know it, or who has forgotten just how it goes. It is a time-tested pastime that never fails to amuse both the young and the old.

Each player is given a long sheet of paper and a pencil, and is told to write down certain information. Each time he writes down the information requested, he folds the top of the paper forward to cover what he has written, and passes the folded sheet to the player on his right, receiving a folded sheet from the player on his left. As can readily be seen, each player adds new information to every sheet of paper without any knowledge of what has previously been written. That is where the fun comes in.

Here is what the players are told the write:

1st. An adjective which is descriptive of a person's appearance.
(Fold and pass)

2nd. The name of a girl, preferably known to all the company.
(Fold and pass)

3rd. The word *met* and an adjective descriptive of a person's character or disposition.
(Fold and pass)

4th. The name of a man, preferably known to all the company.
(Fold and pass)

5th. Where the girl met the man.
(Fold and pass)

6th. The circumstances under which they met.
(Fold and pass)

7th. When they met.
(Fold and pass)

8th. What he said to her.
(Fold and pass)

9th. What she said to him.
(Fold and pass)

10th. What he did.
(Fold and pass)

11th. What she did.
(Fold and pass)

12th. The consequences.
(Fold and pass)

13th. What the neighbors said about the whole affair.

After the last directions have been followed, and the papers have been folded and passed for the thirteenth time, each player in turn unfolds the paper in his possession, and reads aloud what is written on it, filling in such connecting words as may be necessary. The stories that will be heard will be just as ludicrous as the following examples that were actually composed in the course of playing this game.

1. Glamorous Nellie Blain met crazy Joe Bailey back of the grandstand during a fire when she was sixteen. He said, "Let us rest quietly under the shade of the old apple tree." She said, "Go and jump in the lake. I'm a good girl." He telephoned for help. She fell asleep. They were divorced the following December. The neighbors said, "Well, she had it coming to her."

2. Pug-nosed Hildegarde Henry met boisterous Rikki Dooley at the Pennsylvania Railroad Station while the church bells were ringing on the night of the hurricane. He said, "Where do we go from here?" She said, "Mind your own business." He rushed down the hill, screaming for help. She scratched his face and bit his ear. The ship left without them. The neighbors said, "Just as we thought."

88. Cootie

The story is that this game was invented by a soldier in World War I, when cooties caused almost as much unhappiness as shells and bombs. The idea is to draw a picture of a cootie according to the turn of one die.

Each player has a pencil and piece of paper. The first player rolls the die, and the number that comes up tells him what part of the cootie he may draw.

1 is the body. Because the cootie must have a body to which other parts can be added, a player cannot begin to draw his cootie until he has thrown a 1.

2 is the head.

3 is an eye. The cootie must have two eyes.

4 is a feeler, the cootie must have two feelers.

5 is a leg. The cootie must have six legs, three on each side.

6 is the tail.

The first person to complete his cootie calls out, "Cootie." Each person then counts, for his score, the number of parts of his cootie he has completed. Each part counts 1 point; so the winner, with a completed cootie, scores 13 points: 1 for the body, 1 for the head, 2 for the eyes, 2 for the feelers, 6 for the legs, and 1 for the tail.

89. Decapitations

There are many words in the English language which, when shorn of their first letters, spell new words; as, for example, THAT, which, when the first T is erased, spells HAT. When the H in HAT is chopped off AT remains.

Your guests will have fun making up lists of such words and decapitating them as many times as possible. Give each guest a pencil and a piece of paper and see who can make up the longest list of decapitated words. Score 1 point for each successful decapitation.

Here are a few examples of decapitations:

brow, row
coat, oat, at
wheat, heat,
   eat, at
cloves, loves
chit, hit, it
blowing, lowing,
   owing, wing
player, layer
meat, eat, at

90. The Drawing Game

This is a comical game that will be enjoyed by both those who have artistic talent and those who have not.

The guests are divided into two or three teams, and a leader is chosen for each team. The leaders are each given a sheet of paper and a pencil, and are told secretly to draw a picture of a specified object, such as an egg-beater, a lemon-squeezer, a galosh, a zipper, a roller-skate, etc. The leaders rush back to their respective teams and begin drawing the picture. The other members of the teams watch their own leaders and try to guess as quickly as possible the name of the object that is being drawn. The first team to guess correctly wins and scores 5 points. A new leader is then chosen for each team, and a new object is assigned to the new leaders to draw.

It is important to explain at the start that the less artistic the pictures are, the more fun there will be for everyone.

Instead of being told to draw an object, the leaders may be told to illustrate a title or a quotation.

91. Drawing the Invisible

This is a variation of the Drawing Game, and is every bit as amusing. It is played by couples instead of teams.

Each couple sits in chairs, back to back. The man is given a pencil, a sheet of paper, and something that can be used as a drawing board (a tray, book, piece of heavy cardboard, or something of the kind). The girl is given an object, any object not too large, such as a penknife, a box of matches, a slipper, a hat, a pair of scissors, or what have you. Now, without telling her partner what the object is which she has been given, she describes it to him in terms of shape, size, lines, etc.; and, following her directions, he draws a picture of the to-him-invisible object as best he can.

When each picture is finished, it is signed with the names of the couples responsible for it, and put on exhibition. The couple responsible for the picture judged to resemble most closely its model wins. Needless to say, the objects to be drawn must be kept from the view of the artists.

92. Guesswork

Arrange on a table 10 or a dozen different objects, to each of which is attached a card on which is written a question, asking for specific information which no one would be expected to know regarding the object. The objects and questions should be similar to these:

OBJECT	QUESTION
A pint jar of black beans	How many beans are in the jar?
A dictionary	How many pages are in the dictionary?
A cigarette box not wholly filled	How many cigarettes are in the box?
A sofa cushion or pillow	How much does it weigh?
A small ball of twine	How many feet of twine are in the ball?
A partly filled box of kitchen matches	How many matches are in the box?
A stick of wood	How many inches long is it?
A pitcher partly filled with water	How many pints of water are in it?
An incomplete pack of cards	How many cards are in the pack?
Candle in a candlestick	How many inches is it from the table to the end of the wick?

Each player looks at each object, but must not touch it, and, on a piece of paper provided for the purpose, writes down what he thinks is the right answer to each question. After about twenty minutes have expired, read aloud the correct answers, and have the players score their papers, marking 10 points for every correct answer, which will be a great rarity, and 5 points for an answer that is the closest to the correct answer among those given. After all the answers have been compared and scored, the player with the highest score wins.

So that there may be no delay in scoring, the correct answers to all the questions should be ascertained some time before you introduce the game and a record made of them.

93. Hearty Words

Give each of your guests a pencil and paper and have him write down as many single or compound words as he can think of which contain the word *heart*. Allow five minutes for this, and then have each player in turn read his list. As the lists are read the players check on their individual lists the words called. Five points are scored by a player for each word on his list which does not appear on the list of any other player. If no player has a word which another player has not used, the winner is the player who has the greatest number of words on his list. All words must be good English words, and their definitions must be known by the players who use them. Any player may be challenged to give the definition of a word he has used.

Some hearty words are: Heartache, heartbeat, heart block, heartbreak, heartburn, heart disease, hearten, heartfelt, heart-free, heart-heavy, hearthstone, heartily, heartless, heart-rending, heartstrings, heart-struck, heartthrob, etc.

94. How Do You Feel?

The easiest and one of the most amusing ways of playing this game, which can be played in many more ways than one, is to seat your guests around the dining-room table and instruct them to keep their hands always under the table out of view, and also to bend forward, somewhat over the table, so there may be no suspicion of their peeking at their hands.

Now bring in a covered basket containing a dozen different objects, and seat yourself at the head of the table with the basket out of view in your lap. Explain that to the guest on your right you will pass, under the table, one at a time, the objects in your basket. He is to feel each object, guess what it is, and pass it quickly to the guest on his right, who must do likewise. No one is to speak during the proceedings. After the dozen objects have made the journey, under the table, around the group, and have been returned to your basket, each guest, who has been supplied with pencil and paper, is to write down the name of each object. The objects are then displayed and the lists checked. Each person scores one point for each object he has correctly named. The highest score takes the honors.

Any objects may be used for this game, such as the larger half of a carrot, the heart of a head of lettuce, a small piece of emery board, a damp chamois, a dried apricot, a twenty-five cent-piece, a two-inch piece of candle cut evenly at both ends so that the wick does not protrude, a peeled potato, etc., etc.

95. How Do You Rate?

Here is a game that definitely is not recommended for general use. If you are surrounded by very dear friends who are very good sports, you might dare to try it; but you had better make sure first that no one present has concealed on his person a lethal weapon. The perfect group on which to employ the game is, of course, a gathering of your most detested acquaintances.

Arrangements for this game consist of preparing as many slips of paper as there are to be participants. On each slip is written a list of ten qualities or characteristics to be found in a greater or lesser degree in every human being. A master chart is then prepared, listing in a column to the left the ten qualities, and ruling off to the right as many vertical columns as there are to be participants. At the head of each of the vertical columns is written the name of one of the players, a different name in each column.

The game begins when the hostess hands to one of the players a pencil and one of the slips of paper with the ten qualities written on it. "Joe," she says, "step into the next room and rate yourself in respect to these ten qualities, using a scale of ten for each quality—ten being tops, five average, and zero something terrible."

When Joe has closed the door behind him, the other players go to work on Joe's qualities and determine a rating for each one. These ratings are entered on the master chart, under Joe's name. There will be plenty of disagreement, so the final rating to be entered on the master chart should respresent the average. For example, Bill, Jane, and Harry may think Joe's charm rates 8; Mary and Peter strongly argue that it is not worth more than 3; Connie, Horace, Betty, and Paul decide it should be 6; and Liz says, to her way of thinking, it is no better than average and should rate 5. The average of these ratings, or 5.5, is entered on the master chart opposite CHARM in the column headed by Joe's name.

When all of the ten qualities have been rated by the gang in respect to Joe, Joe is called back into the room and asked to read off his own ratings. As he gives his own estimate for each quality he is cheerfully informed how he rates with the gang on that particular quality.

Great sport, isn't it?

Here is an invidious list of qualities for a go at this game. You undoubtedly can think up for yourself a more odious, or pleasanter, list.

Intelligence
Good Looks
Charm
Sportsmanship
Sense of Humor
Generosity
Sex Appeal
Popularity
Good Manners

96. Jumbled Words

Brain-teasing addicts never fail to enjoy untangling jumbled words. Make up a list of 20 or 30 proverbs, maxims, titles of famous books, or names of famous persons and rearrange the letters in each word or name so that they appear to make no sense. Typewrite enough copies of the list to supply every one at the party with a copy. Then give each person a copy and a pencil, and for the next 20 or 30 minutes you will be free to empty the ashtrays, refill the punch bowl, get the refreshments ready, or do any other chores that may be necessary. The one who first unscrambles his complete list wins.

Here are a few jumbled quotations:

ONTI HACE FILE MOES NIRA TUMS LAFL
(Into each life some rain must fall.)

NME THUS RETIH ODORS ATASING A TENGIST NSU
(Men shut their doors against a setting sun.)

LOSOF HURS NI REWEH GALSEN AFRE OT DRATE
(Fools rush in where angels fear to tread.)

RANSPEACAPE REA TEFON GEDICINEV
(Appearances are often deceiving.)

NEHW GYRNA CTONU NET ROBEEF OYU KAPES
(When angry, count ten before you speak.)

ASNORE LOHDUS CRITED DAN TEATIPEP BOYE
(Reason should direct and appetite obey.)

HURTT SI SNERGART NATH NOICFTI
(Truth is stranger than fiction.)

TOFRENU RAFSOV HET LOBD
(Fortune favors the bold.)

OKOL FEEROB UYO PALE
(Look before you leap.)

TREEBT TALE NTAH RENVE
(Better late than never.)

166

97. Picture Biographies

Here, for a group of good-natured, fun-loving game-sters, is a fun-packed activity, which combines history with prophecy. But, before you introduce it, you had better screen your guests to make sure that among them there are no hypersensitive introverts, or for that matter, sharptoothed backbiters. When you play with picture biographies, you play with atoms, and you ought to be prepared to have one split without warning. The possibilities of this game for originality, wit, humor, and hurt feelings are limitless.

First, you will have to procure enough blank-books, not larger than 9" by 12", to supply one to each of your guests. These you can easily make yourself out of sheets of light wrapping paper 22" by 34". Fold each sheet in half, the narrow (22") way; then fold it in half again, the narrow way; and then fold it once more in half, but this time the long way. Now, with a knife, or paper cutter, cut, as you would the leaves in an uncut book, the two folds running the long way, and the two folds running the narrow way. You will then have a sixteen-page booklet, 8½" by 11". With thread or cotton stitch and tie these pages together where they fold.

You will also have to have on hand a generous supply of different, illustrated magazines: *Life, Look, Saturday Evening Post, Collier's, Ladies' Home Journal, McCall's, Parents', Good Housekeeping,* etc.

Seat your guests on the floor or at the dining-room table and provide each with one of the blank-books or booklets, a pair of scissors, a tube of musilage, and a few colored crayons. In their midst spread the magazines.

Now give to each of the men the name of a different girl, and to each of the girls the name of a different man, all of whom are present, and tell each to make a picture biography of the person whose name you have given him or her by selecting and cutting out pictures from the magazines and pasting them in his or her blank-book, adding, with crayon, appropriate captions and details.

The first (outside) page of the blank-book bears the title of the biography, appropriately decorated. Then each of the other pages illustrate and explain a different incident in the past and future life of the subject. One scrapbook, for instance, might deal with these topics: It's a Boy (or Girl)! First Tooth, First Words, School Days, Puppy Love, Graduation, First Job, True Love, Marriage, First Quarrel, Children, Favorite Pastime, Greatest Achievement, Retirement, Epitaph.

Prizes of no consequence (razor blades for a man and a dress-ornament ax or anvil hammer for a girl) may be given to the one who first finishes a scrapbook and the one whose scrapbook is judged to be cleverest.

98. Scribble Drawing

Persons of all ages, colors, creeds, political beliefs, and degrees of intelligence will have fun with this game, which is a particularly suitable diversion for small groups. Each player is given a sheet of paper and a pencil, and is instructed to scribble on the paper a continuous line of any kind desired, bent, curved, crooked, zigzag, or what he thinks up. It is better not to make it too long. When each player has scribbled his line on his paper, he passes his paper to the player on his left, receiving a paper from the player on his right. When all the papers have been passed, each player completes on the paper now in his possession an original picture in which the scribble appearing on the paper must be made an integral part.

In the end all the drawings may be put on exhibition and a vote taken on which is the most original, which is the most artistic, and which is the funniest.

99. See A, B, C

This can be recommended as a good pre-party activity. It will reveal whether or not your guests can see what they are looking at.

Pin on the walls half a dozen pictures of scenes—a street, a country store, a beach party, a car at a filling station, etc. These may be cut from magazines. The larger the pictures are, the better will they serve your purpose. Clearly letter each picture; A, B, and so on.

Upon his arrival, give each guest a pencil and a piece of paper, and instruct him to look at each picture, and, as he examines it, to write down as many objects as he can find which begin with the letter by which the picture is identified. At the first picture all of the objects in that picture which are spelled with an A for the first letter are written down; at the second picture all of the objects beginning with B; and at the third picture all of the objects beginning with C.

The winner is the person who has listed accurately the greatest number of objects.

100. Slogan Guessing

Slogan Guessing can be conducted in several different ways. First, a list of 20 or 30 well-known advertising slogans should be prepared, and a sufficient number of copies made to provide one for each of your guests. Each guest is required to write opposite each slogan the name of the product with which it is associated. The guest who first identifies all of the slogans wins, or the one who identifies the greatest number of the slogans within a period of 10 or 15 minutes.

A second way of proceeding is to write the slogans on numbered cards and hang the cards on the wall or on a screen where all can see them. Then give each guest a blank sheet of paper and a pencil, and tell him to number the products he writes down to correspond with the numbers on the slogan cards.

Still another method is to paste on cards pictures of products clipped from magazine and newspaper advertisements, numbering each picture for identification. The cards are then hung on the wall, and the guests are instructed to write down the slogans which are associated with each product, numbering them to correspond with the picture numbers.

Here is a list of old and recent slogans which nearly every one should know:

99-44/100% Pure *(Ivory Soap)*
Blues as It Washes *(Rinso Blue)*
The Champagne of Ginger Ales *(Canada Dry)*

Babies Are Our Business . . . Our *Only* Business
   (Gerber's Baby Foods)
Say It With Flowers *(Society of American Florists)*
At the Sign of the Flying Red Horse *(Mobile Gasoline)*
Hasn't Scratched Yet *(Bon Ami)*
Breakfast of Champions *(Wheaties)*
The Dash that Makes the Dish! *(A-1 Sauce)*
Progress Is Our Most Important Product *(General Electric)*
Look Sharp, Feel Sharp, Be Sharp *(Gillette Blue Blades)*
Come See, Come Save *(A&P Stores)*
Fresh Up With— *(Seven-Up)*
The Friendliest Drink on Earth *(Coca-Cola)*
Finer Filter. Finer Flavor *(Winston Cigarettes)*
From Contented Cows *(Carnation Milk)*
Chases Dirt *(Old Dutch Cleanser)*
As Strong As the Rock of Gibralter *(Prudential Insurance Company)*
The Greatest Name in Perfume *(Caron)*
Covers the Earth *(Sherwin-Williams Paint)*
It's Toasted *(Lucky Strike Cigarettes)*
World's Most Experienced Airline *(Pan American)*
Good to the Last Drop *(Maxwell House Coffee)*
When It Rains It Pours *(Morton's Salt)*
Once a Day . . . *Every Day* . . . Soup! *(Campbell Soups)*
It's the Next Best Thing to a Dishwashing Machine
   (Lux Liquid Detergent)

101. Smelly Business

This test of the sense of smell will provide much merriment. Obtain from your local druggist half a dozen one-ounce medicine bottles without labels. Fill each bottle with a different liquid that has a distinctive odor, such as bay-rum, iodine, turpentine, rubbing alcohol, coffee, tea, ammonia, citronella, vinegar, and any perfume. Give each of your guests a pencil and a piece of paper and ask him to write down what is contained in each bottle after he has smelled the contents. Of course, the winner is the one who smells best. In other words, the one who identifies the contents of the greatest number of bottles.

102. Telegrams

Who hasn't struggled with the problem of writing a sensible telegram limited to ten words and been convinced that the ordeal is a top ranking test of mental agility and vocabulary mastery? Be that as it may, in reality it is a third-rate test compared with writing a sensible telegram in which every word must begin with a certain predetermined letter and none other. That is a challenge to stimulating mental activity which very few of your friends and acquaintances will refuse to accept and enjoy.

Supply your guests with pencils and paper. Tell them to write down a word you will give them. The word should have some significance for the occasion of your party. If you are giving a birthday party, the word could be BIRTHDAY. If you are giving a Valentine's party, the word could be SWEETHEART.

When all have written down the word, explain that each one is to write a sensible, but not necessarily a serious, telegram, using the letters of the word, in the order in which they are employed to spell the word, as the first letters of the words of the telegram.

If you were having an Easter party, you might use the word EASTER for this game. In which case some one might write for his telegram, *Eggs Are Served To Early Risers*, and another guest might write, *Elderly Aunt Slept Through Easter Recital*.

103. United Nations Flags

A very good guessing game which is especially appropriate for a patriotic party or nationality party, employs the flags (or colored pictures of the flags) of all the nations belonging to the United Nations. The flags are incorporated in the room decorations, and each flag has a number attached to its staff. The guests are given pencils and paper, and are told to find and identify every flag. Whoever succeeds in finding and identifying all of the flags first is the winner.

104. Who's Who

How many famous persons of the day could you or your friends recognize if you should meet them on the street?

This game will give your guests some idea of their familiarity with the famous and provide a number of surprises for them.

This is what you will have to do before your guests arrive. Clip from recent pictorial magazines pictures of persons who have received widespread publicity in newspaper stories, magazine articles, radio broadcasts, and newsreels, removing from each picture all descriptive matter that might disclose who the person is. Paste these pictures, of which there should be at least twenty, on large sheets of cardboard or Bristol board and hang them on the wall where they can readily be examined by your guests. The pictures must be numbered in consecutive order.

Provide the guests with pencils and paper and tell them to write down the correct name of the famous person shown in each picture, numbering each of his guesses to correspond with the picture it applies to. After a reasonable time, 15 or 20 minutes, has elapsed, read aloud the correct names of the characters in the pictures in the order in which they are numbered, so that your guests can check their guesses and determine who has made the largest number of correct guesses. To him the laurels.

105. Zippee

This is an exciting game that is becoming more and more popular. It is played with five dice, and a score sheet for each player. Any number of persons can play the game.

First of all, each player prepares his own score sheet, which is arranged as follows:

Bill Doakes

Games	1	2	3	4	5	6	7	8
1								
2								
3								
4								
5								
6								
Total								
Bonus								
Short Straight								
Long Straight								
Full House								
Best Hand								
Zippee								
Grand Total								

It will be seen from the score sheet that each player has twelve opportunities to score in each game. In the upper half of the score sheet the numbers 1 through 6 refer to the pips on the dice. To score in this section a player must roll at least three of any one of these numbers.

This is how he plays. He picks up all five dice, shakes

173

them, and throws them on the table. He then decides which of the six numbers he will play for. Supposing his dice on the first roll show two fours, two twos, and a six. He has a choice of playing for twos, fours, or sixes. If he decides to play for the fours, he picks up the twos and the six, and leaves the two fours on the table. He then rolls the three dice he picked up. Supposing he rolls two sixes and a two, he will then have on the table the two fours he left there and the two sixes and the two which he got on his second roll. He is permitted only one more roll of the dice. He must now make up his mind whether to roll for the fours, the sixes, or a Full House. A Full House is one pair and three of a kind. In this case it would be either three sixes and two fours or three fours and two sixes. If he chooses to play for the Full House, he picks up the two and throws that for his last roll. If it turns up a four or a six, he makes his Full House, and scores the total number of pips showing on the five dice in the box opposite Full House on the lower half of the score sheet, in this case 24 or 26, depending on whether he got three fours and two sixes or three sixes and two fours.

If he had decided to roll for the fours instead of for the Full House, he would have picked up the two sixes and the two and thrown them for his third and last roll. In this case, had the dice turned up a two, a four, and a five, he would have made his fours and would have scored in the box opposite the number 4 in the upper half of the score sheet the total number of pips on the dice showing four, or, in this case, 12. Had he rolled, in his three chances, four fours, he would have scored 16.

After his third roll, the player records his score on his score sheet and passes the dice to the player on his left, who proceeds as the first player did, selecting after each roll what dice he wishes to roll on his second and third try. When he has completed his three rolls, he records his score on his score sheet, and then passes the dice to the player on his left. So the game continues until all fourteen boxes on the score sheets of each of the players have been filled. The player having the highest Grand Total wins.

Now, there is a gimmick in this game which provides the interest, excitement, and tension. A player may score only once in each of the boxes on the score sheet. For instance, if he has made his threes and entered his score, he cannot again score threes, even if later he should roll four threes. And here is the gimmick: if a player fails to score, or is unable to enter a score because the appropriate box has already been occupied, he must mark an X in one of the remaining vacant boxes on his score sheet, and that box is considered filled and cannot again be scored in.

If a player's total score for the first six boxes on his score sheet amounts to 63 or better, he receives a bonus of 50, which is entered in the box opposite Bonus. If the total for these six boxes is less than 63, an X is marked in the Bonus box.

For a Short Straight the dice must show a one, a two, a three, a four, and a five; and for a Long Straight they must show a two, a three, a four, a five, and a six. A Short Straight counts 15, and a Long Straight counts 20.

At any time during a game a player may elect to call any throw he makes a Best Hand. For example, if he should throw four sixes and a five in two rolls and he had already scored sixes, he could call this his best hand and score 29 in the box opposite Best Hand. The Best Hand scores all the pips showing on the five dice. The highest score for a Best Hand is 36, and the lowest is 5.

A Zippee is five of a kind, and counts 50, which is scored in the box opposite Zippee.

The sum of all seven boxes in the lower half of the score sheet is the Grand Total and final score. X's, of course, do not count.

Although a player is permitted three rolls at each turn, he does not have to roll three times. For instance, should he on his first roll throw three fives and two sixes, he could immediately score a Full House, and surrender the dice, and await his next turn. Likewise, if in two rolls he turned up a Long Straight, he is allowed to forego the third roll and immediately score the Long Straight.

7. Stunts

106. Apple or Flour

Here is one of the best of all the Halloween stunts, so dear to the hearts of old and young. Hang from the center of the ceiling, or from the center of a doorway, a string, at the end of which is fastened a stick, or cane, in such a way that it remains parallel to the floor. From one end of the stick suspend a thin cloth bag filled with flour, and from the other end suspend a ripe, juicy, red apple. Now stand each guest in turn close to this contraption, and start the apple and bag of flour spinning around for all they are worth, in merry-go-round fashion. Then tell the guest to step in and grab the apple with his teeth. If he succeeds in biting the apple, he will be fortunate in all matters of love; but, if he fails, he will be unfortunate indeed, and, incidentally, will require considerable dusting off.

107. Bottoms Up

This is a puzzle game for table fun. It requires 3 empty tumblers.

Stand the first tumbler right-side up on the table. Next to it, place the second tumbler upside down. And next to the second tumbler, place the third tumbler right-side up. Now challenge any one present to bring all three tumblers into the upside down (or bottoms-up) position in three moves, explaining that each move consists of turning over any two of the tumblers. Two tumblers, no more and no less, must be turned over at each move and only three moves are allowed.

Here is the know-how. First move, turn over the second and third tumblers; second move, turn over the first and third tumblers; and, third and last move, turn over the second and third tumblers again. Now all three tumblers will be bottoms-up.

176

Simple it is, but try it on a group of friends and see how many can figure it out for themselves, even after you have demonstrated it for them once.

108. Candle Blowing

This is an old Halloween stunt, but it is suitable for other occasions, and it is always amusing. Line up on a table seven lighted candles. Six or eight feet from the table have one of your guests stand, facing the candles. Now blindfold the guest, turn him completely around three times, and tell him to walk to the table and blow three times at the candle flames. He is allowed three blows and no more. If he blows out all of the candles, we are told, he will be married within the year. If he is married already, he will never be divorced. If he fails to blow out any of the candles, he will never marry. If he is already married, he will be divorced within the year. If 1, 2, 3, 4, 5, or 6 candles are left burning, they indicate the number of years before he will marry, if unmarried; or, if married, the number of years he will remain married to his present wife.

109. Cardinal Puff

Whether you drink to the toast of Cardinal Puff with snake medicine, schnapps, soda pop, or just plain water, the results will be just as befuddling, and you need not be surprised to learn the next day that more than one of your playmates were seen to be acting very oddly on the way home from your gathering.

As you must introduce the toast of Cardinal Puff, you should practice it well before you let your friends in on it.

In front of your seated guests place a card table and a chair. On the table place a glass filled with a beverage, and next to the glass have ready a plentiful supply of the beverage for refilling purposes.

Stand at the chair and explain to your guests that you are about to teach them the famous toast of Cardinal Puff and that they are to follow your speech and actions with the greatest possible concentration, so that they will be able, each in his turn, to drink to the toast of Cardinal Puff after you.

Now follow the following routine exactly:

1. Make a very courtly bow, and say: "This is the toast of Cardinal Puff. Here's how!"

2. Sit on the chair at the table.

3. Pick up the glass between the thumb and first finger of your right hand.

4. Drink one draft from the glass.

5. Tap the glass once on the table, as you put it down.

6. Strike the edge of the table once with the first finger of your right hand.

7. Strike the edge of the table once with the first finger of your left hand.

8. Strike your right knee with the first finger of your right hand.

9. Strike your left knee with the first finger of your left hand.

10. Stamp on the floor once with your right foot.

11. Stamp on the floor once with your left foot.

12. Stand up and bow twice in a very courtly manner and say: "Here's how! Here's how!"

13. Sit down.

14. Pick up the glass between the thumb and next two fingers of your right hand.

15. Drink two drafts from the glass.

16. Tap the glass twice on the table, as you put it down.

17. Strike the edge of the table twice with the first two fingers of your right hand.

18. Strike the edge of the table twice with the first two fingers of your left hand.

19. Strike your right knee twice with the first two fingers of your right hand.

20. Strike your left knee twice with the first two fingers of your left hand.

21. Stamp on the floor twice with your right foot.

22. Stamp on the floor twice with your left foot.

23. Stand up and bow three times in a very courtly manner, and say: "Here's how! Here's how! Here's how!"

24. Sit down.

25. Pick up the glass between the thumb and next *three* fingers of your right hand.

26. Drink three times from the glass, *emptying* it.

27. Tap the glass three times on the table, as you put it down.

28. Strike the edge of the table three times with the first three fingers of your right hand.

29. Strike the edge of the table three times with the first three fingers of your left hand.

30. Strike your right knee three times with the first three fingers of your right hand.

31. Strike your left knee three times with the first three fingers of your left hand.

32. Stamp on the floor three times with your right foot.

33. Stamp on the floor three times with your left foot.

34. Stand up and say, "That's how."

Now point to one of the guests and say, "Let's see you drink to the toast of Cardinal Puff."

The guest at whom you point must then take over, with a freshly filled glass. He must follow the routine as demonstrated by you, exactly as you did it. If he makes a mistake, you may do either of two things: disqualify him and have another guest take his place; or refill his glass and tell him to start over again.

As you can guess, this is a very satisfactory game with which to conclude an evening's entertainment.

110. Exchanging Wine for Water

Few stunts can surpass this one for eeriness. Even while you are watching it you suspect you are being tricked in some manner.

The stunt is performed with two matching wine glasses. One of these you fill to the brim with water and the other you fill to the brim with red wine. Now you explain that you can put these two glasses together in such a way that the wine, of its own accord, will change places with the water. When the operation has been completed the wine will occupy the glass previously occupied by the water, and the water will be in the glass previously occupied by the wine. If any one wants to bet you it can't be done, don't hesitate to take him up in any amount he is willing to risk.

To perform this stunt, first cover the glass holding the water with a piece of heavy paper or very thin cardboard, large enough to cover the glass with half an inch all around to spare. Now, holding the paper against the glass with the palm of your hand, quickly turn the glass upside down. You can now release the paper and it will cling to the rim of the glass and prevent the water from spilling out. Next, without removing the paper from the inverted glass, place the glass on top of the wine glass filled with wine, in such a manner that the rim of the upper glass is directly above the rim of the lower glass at every point. The upper glass may not at any point overlap the under glass. This is very important.

Now comes the ticklish manipulation. With great care, withdraw slightly the paper from between the two glasses until there is a small space of not more than a quarter of an inch in width between the edge of the paper and the rims of the glasses. That is all you have to do; the water and wine do the rest. To the amazement of the spectators, the water will slowly descend down through the opening you made by slightly withdrawing the paper partition and will force the wine to rise through the same opening into the upper glass. This process will continue until all the water has settled in the lower glass, formerly occupied by the wine, and all of the wine has taken possession of the water glass.

The problem of how to separate the two glasses, after this stunt is done, without drenching everything with the wine and the water is left to you to work out! The best advice is to perform this stunt on a waterproof tray, and never mind what happens when you separate the two glasses.

111. Forfeits

Sometimes it is more fun to make the losers pay a forfeit than to award a prize to the winners. But be careful not to require too many forfeits. Forfeits should be introduced as something of a surprise. Employed too often they become tiresome.

The following forfeits are among the more popular ones.

Act like a girl confronted with a mouse.

Hoot like an owl.

Blow out a candle while blindfolded.

Say the alphabet backwards.

Keep yawning until you can make some one else yawn.

Poke yourself through a curtain ring. (Put your finger through the ring and poke yourself.)

Sew a patch on the seat of a man's trousers while he lies across your lap.

Feed your partner a banana while you and your partner are both blindfolded.

While blindfolded find a collar-button placed on the floor.

Kiss a book inside and outside without opening it. (Kiss the book; go out the front door and kiss it again.)

Put one hand where the other hand can't touch it. (Touch one of your elbows with one of your hands.)

Impersonate a city policeman doing traffic duty at a busy intersection.

Say three nice things about yourself without using the pronoun "I."

Push a peanut across the floor with your nose.

Facing the ceiling, crawl across the room on your hands and feet, going in the direction toward which your head points.

Lie on the floor on your back, with your hands at your sides, and, after having someone balance a quarter on your nose, work the quarter off your nose without moving your head or touching the coin with your hands. You can wiggle your nose and make all the funny faces you want to, but you mustn't move your head.

Drink a glass of water while lying on your back.

Bow to the wittiest, kneel to the prettiest, and kiss the one you love best.

Hop across the room backward on your left foot, while holding the ankle of your right foot with your left hand.

Recite the alphabet, omitting all the vowels.

Name in the right order the months of the year which have less than 31 days. (February, September, April, June, and November.)

Hold your nose with your right hand and your right ear with your left hand. Quickly change the positions of your hands, so that the left hand holds your nose and your right hand holds your left ear. Quickly change your hands back to their first position. Repeat 12 times.

Pat the top of your head with your right hand while rubbing your stomach, circular fashion, with your left hand.

112. Guessing Your Girth

If you want to learn what that pretty, slim girl friend of yours thinks of her figure and what that middle-aged pal of yours thinks of his, this stunt will tell you, much to the mirth of those who witness it, and much to the astonishment of the victim.

All you need to perform this stunt is a length of stout cord about four feet long. Make a circle on the floor with this cord, and, at the point on the circle where the two ends of the cord meet, cross the two ends. Now ask your victim to step up and keep his eyes on the circle. Explain that you are going to diminish the circumference of the circle by slowly pulling, in opposite directions, the ends of the cord. Instruct the victim to order you to stop diminishing the circle when he believes the circumference of the circle has reached the same dimension as the circumference of his midriff.

When you are told to stop, pick up the cord, holding it very carefully in each hand at the point where the cord is crossed. Now throw the loop over the victim and show him how far wrong he was in his guess. If his size was really as big as he thought it was, he would have something worth worrying about.

113. Heaving in the Modern Manner

This stunt is an old favorite. It is reminiscent of the very ancient custom of *heaving* which was practiced in the olden days at Easter, when gay blades sallied forth, made chairs with their crossed hands, and, catching pretty girls in these chairs, heaved them aloft three times.

Seat a man in a straight-backed, armless chair, and tell him that, with supernatural aid, he will be lifted from the chair by five female fingers, no more and no less. Make it clear to everyone present that at a signal all, including the man to be lifted, must take a deep breath, at one and the same time. Explain that if they do this and concentrate their thoughts on the success of the venture, the venture must succeed, otherwise it must fail. Do not fail to emphasize this point.

Instruct the man in the chair to keep his head rigid and slightly bent forward, and to keep his hands clasped together in his lap, and his elbows close to his sides. Now station two girls on each side of the chair and two in back of the chair. Then instruct the girls on either side of the chair each to put one finger under the nearest knee of the man sitting in the chair, and the two girls in back of the chair each to put one finger under a different armpit of the man in the chair. Then ask a fifth girl to step up beside the chair and place one finger under the chin of the man. The gentleman in the chair will now have a girl's finger under his chin, one under each armpit, and one under each knee.

The next thing to do is to remind every one that at the count of three each and every one must take a deep breath, and at that very second the five girls whose fingers are in contact with the man in the chair must raise their fingers simultaneously. If every one follows the directions exactly, the man in the chair will so suddenly be heaved aloft that the girls doing the heaving will squeal with astonishment and momentarily forget that the fate of the man is in their fingers. This will result in a crisis, the resolution of which no one can foretell. The one thing you may be sure of is that the only discomfort that the spectators will suffer will be caused by too much laughter.

114. High Hat

An absurdly humorous guessing game that is just right for winding up a party is this test of judgment.

Hang along a wall a long sheet of paper, so that one edge touches the floor and the other is at least two feet above the floor. Tell your guests that they must know a good deal about their hats, but that you doubt very much that they know how high their hats are. Ask each guest to mark on the sheet of paper you have hung on the wall where he thinks the top of his hat will reach, when the hat has been placed on the floor beside the sheet of paper. With a pencil each guest indicates on the paper, with a line and his initials, how high he thinks his hat is. When all have done this, each guest is requested to get his hat and place it on the floor next to the paper where he has made his mark. The relationships of the altitudes of the hats to the marks on the paper will be astonishing.

After the best guesser has been determined and appropriately rewarded, the guests will find themselves hats-in-hands, and, if they are smart, they will go home.

115. Is This It?

You can easily awe a group with this mystifying performance, which is as simple to do as podding peas.

Send one of the group out of the room and close the door behind him, so that he can neither see nor hear what goes on in the room. Ask those remaining in the room to agree on some object in the room which the person sent out will be asked to identify when he returns. Call the person back into the room and say to him: "I shall touch various articles in this room, one of which has been selected for you to identify. Please tell me when I touch the article selected for identification." After touching a number of different articles, you finally touch the article selected, and the person who is to identify the article immediately says, "That is it."

Of course, the person you choose to leave the room is your confederate and is in the know. You have previously told him secretly that immediately after you touch something black, you will touch the article he is to identify. Pretty childish, eh what? But just see how long it takes the gang to discover the secret.

While performing this feat, you must take care not to touch anything that is black unless you immediately after touch the article to be identified. It goes without saying that the signal may be changed. The signal could be to touch something red, or to touch something that has legs (such as a table, chair, or another person).

116. Magic Addition

If you want to show your guests how smart you are at mathematics, play this trick on them.

Ask one of your guests to write down a number of five digits, any number he wants. Now tell your guest that you can write down, in advance, what the sum will be of that number added to four other numbers of five digits each, if you are permitted to write the third and fifth numbers. In other words, the guest will write the second number to be added, you will write the third, the guest will write the fourth, and you will write the fifth. When these numbers are totaled the result will be the number you wrote in advance.

This is how it works. The guest chooses and writes the number 31246. You tell him the result of the addition to this and four other five digit numbers, of which you will give the third and fifth, will be 231244. The guest then selects for the second number 32416; you give for the third number 67583; he selects for the fourth number 23234; and you write for the fifth number 76765. These five numbers added together equals 231244, the number you announced in advance.

$$
\begin{array}{r}
31246 \\
32416 \\
67583 \\
23234 \\
76765 \\
\hline
231244
\end{array}
$$

It is extremely simple. The total can be told by writing down 2, then the first four digits of the first number chosen by the guest, and finally the number that is two less than the last digit of the guest's number. In the case cited above, the guest's first number was 31246, so the total of the addition will be 2, and then the first four digits of the number, which are 3124, and finally two less than the last digit, which is $6 - 2 = 4$. The whole number will be 231244.

To be right every time will depend upon the numbers you select. After the guest has written the second number, which may be any number at all containing five digits, be sure that each digit you write for the third number, when added to the corresponding digit of the second number, will equal nine. For example, in the case cited above, $3 + 6 = 9$, $8 + 1 = 9$, $5 + 4 = 9$, $7 + 2 = 9$, and $6 + 3 = 9$. Follow the same principles in writing the fifth number. Each digit of the fifth number when added to the corresponding digit of the fourth number must total 9. In the case cited above, $5 + 4 = 9$, $6 + 3 = 9$, $7 + 2 = 9$, $6 + 3 = 9$, and $7 + 2 = 9$.

That is all there is to it. But it is exceedingly mystifying to those not in the know.

There are complications to watch out for. If the original number chosen by your guest ends with a 1 or 0, to find the total you want, subtract 2 from the number and place a 2 at the left of the result. For example, if the guest selects for his first number, 65451, subtract 2 from this number, which will give you, 65449, and place a 2 at the left, which will give you, 265449.

117. Magic Eight Pile

Deceptively select the four eights from a pack of cards and place them in a pile, face down, on a table. Then select any eight cards from the pack without revealing the number selected or their values, and place them in another pile, face down, on the table. Now tell someone that you will hypnotize him to point to a particular one of the two piles.

Write on a piece of paper, *You will point to the eight pile.* Fold the paper over and hand it to your victim. Then tell him to point to one of the piles. After he has pointed, tell him to read what you have written. Then, if he pointed to the eight-card pile, pick up the pile and count aloud the cards, keeping them face down. Then count aloud the cards in the other pile, keeping them face down. This will prove to him that you made him point to the *eight pile*, the pile which had eight cards. If he pointed to the four-card pile, turn the cards in that pile face up, and show him that he pointed to the *eight pile*, the pile containing nothing only eights. You win either way.

118. No!

Here is a simple, but very effective stunt, which is useful as a time filler, or to launch a program of stunts.

The hostess says she bets that she can make at least one of her guests say, "No!" when she wants him or her to say it. She then asks for three or four volunteers to accept her challenge. Because everyone knows it is not necessary to say *no* unless one wants to, several persons will accept the challenge. The hostess lines these volunteers up in front of her, and looks at them inquisitively. Suddenly she says, "Oh, you know this trick, don't you?" Ninety-nine times out of a hundred, at least one of the volunteers will answer right back, "No."

And that's that.

119. Picking Two Coins Off a Glass

Balance two nickels or quarters, opposite each other, on the rim of a high-ball glass. Then challenge any one to step up and pick both coins off the glass *at exactly the same time*, using only the thumb and index finger of one hand. As you issue your challenge suggest how the stunt might be done by holding a thumb over one of the coins and the index finger of the same hand over the other coin, and, raising your hand, pinch the thumb and index finger together, exactly as if you had picked up both coins between them.

As with most stunts, the solution of this problem is obvious (once you know it) and simple. Hold a thumb over one coin and the index finger of the same hand over the other coin. Then bring the thumb and index finger down on top of the coins at exactly the same time, tipping both coins outward, and sliding them down the sides of the glass, until they are about midway from top to bottom. Now squeeze your thumb and index finger together, drawing them, with the coins, around the sides of the glass, towards you, until the two coins meet, when they both can be picked off the glass at one and the same time.

120. Prize Cards

Any number of players up to 48 can participate in this wicked game of chance, which for nerve-racking suspense beats everything. It is played with 2 packs of cards, distinguishable by color or design, and a supply of poker chips.

First, the poker chips are distributed among the players in any way that is satisfactory to all.

To play the game, the dealer picks up the first pack of cards, and from it deals 4 cards, which he places in a row, face down, in the center of the table. The players then each place 3 chips in the center of the table, and these chips the dealer distributes unequally on the 4 cards, in such a manner that one of the 4 cards will have on it considerably more chips than are on any of the other cards. For example, if there are 12 players, 36 chips would be placed on the center of the table and the dealer could distribute these so that the first card would have 14 chips, the second 10, the third 7 and the fourth 5.

After the chips have been divided among the 4 cards, the dealer takes up the second pack of cards and deals them to the players so that each player receives an equal number of cards. If any cards are left over after the deal has been completed, these cards are auctioned off, one at a time, to the highest bidder. The proceeds from the auction are then added to the chips on the 4 cards on the center of the table.

Now the fun begins. The dealer picks up the 48 cards left in the first pack of cards and places them one at a time face up on the table. As he does this a player who holds the corresponding card in his hand places it on top of the card turned up by the dealer. If, for instance, the dealer places a Jack of Spades on the table, the player who holds a Jack of Spades places it on top of the dealer's Jack. This continues until the 48 cards of the first pack have been matched with 48 cards from the second pack.

When this has been done there will be left among the players 4 cards of the second pack, and these 4 cards, obviously, will correspond with the 4 cards from the first pack which are face down on the table under the chips.

Now comes the payoff.

The dealer first turns up the card upon which is the smallest number of chips, and the player holding the corresponding card in his hand immediately claims the chips. Then the dealer turns face up the card having upon it the next smallest number of chips and pays off the player who holds the corresponding card. And so it goes until the dealer has turned up the last card which holds the Grand Prix.

After each payoff, the deal should change hands, so that every player will have an opportunity to deal the cards and distribute the chips. Should no one buy the leftover cards at the end of a deal, they are discarded, and, if any of them correspond to a prize card, the chips on that prize card are left on the card for the next deal.

121. Putting Your Finger on It

Here is a sixty-four-thousand-dollar stunt, if introduced at the right moment, without warning, and without any prveious elaborate preparation.

When the party needs a shot in the arm, or between games, or at some other critical moment, you say, "You know, I am something of a mind reader. I'd like to bet that, if some one writes something on a sheet of paper while I am out of the room, and places the slip of paper, folded on a table, when I return to the room, I can tell all of you what is on the paper."

Ask a person to write a long, complicated message, or quotation, on a piece of paper, and let everyone else in the room know what it is he has written. Then leave the room. When the paper has been written on, folded, and placed on the table, you are called back into the room.

On your return, ask everyone to concentrate on what appears on the paper. Then walk over to the paper, and, with one finger touch the folded paper, and assume a look of great concentration. Suddenly say, "Oh! I have it! The paper has on it my finger." Sure enough, that is right.

122. Removing a Bill from Under a Bottle

Lay flat on the floor, or a table, a dollar bill, and on the center of it balance upside down a "pop" bottle. Now ask any one present to remove the bill from under the bottle without touching the bottle or upsetting it. It doesn't seem possible, but it really is very simple. All you have to do is to roll up the bill. Beginning at a narrow end of the bill, turn over the edge of the bill, and, keeping your fingers at the side edges of the bill, continue to roll the bill over. When the roll comes in contact with the top of the bottle, proceed slowly, and the roll will gently push the head of the bottle along in front of it, until the bottle is finally pushed off the bill. There is no need for your fingers to touch the bottle.

A more spectacular stunt of the same nature can be demonstrated with two "pop" bottles or beer bottles. First, be sure both bottles are absolutely dry. Place one bottle right-side up, and over the top of it lay a dollar bill. Now, very carefully, balance the second bottle, upside down, on the dollar bill directly over the top of the first bottle. The problem is to remove the bill from between the two bottles without upsetting either of the bottles. No sir, you don't roll up the bill. The way you do it is to hold very steadily in your left hand one end of the bill, and, with the extended index finger of your right hand, very swiftly strike the bill from above, about midway between your left hand and the bottles. If you hold your right hand steady and grasp the bill firmly, and if you strike the bill with a swift downward stroke, the bill will slip from between the bottles so quickly that the setup of the bottles will not be disturbed.

In setting up the bottles be sure that the rim of the top of the upper bottle is directly above the rim of the top of the lower bottle, so that, when the bill is removed, both rims will meet each other at every point.

123. Spear the Ring

This stunt, which sounds simple enough, will give any one who tries it one of the biggest surprises he has ever experienced.

Suspend a small curtain ring from the ceiling or from the center of a doorway, so that the ring is head-high from the ground. Ask each guest in turn to stand ten feet from the ring. Give him a pair of opera glasses and instruct him to keep the opera glasses to his eyes all the time during the performance of the stunt. Now tell him to sight the curtain ring through the glasses, and, when he has it in focus, to walk quickly, without hesitation, up to the ring, halt, raise his right hand, and immediately put the first finger of his right hand through the ring. It is a very good bet indeed that he will fall short of the mark.

The person's actions must be quick and continuous and he must not raise his hand until he has stopped at the place where he thinks the ring is suspended. One jab with his finger at the ring is all that is allowed.

124. Spoon Portraiture

Here is an old, old favorite, so be sure to ask your guests if they are familiar with it before you introduce this stunt. If only one or two of the guests know how it is done, ask them to do it or to help you. It requires two persons who are in the know. One of these two leaves the room. The other asks for a volunteer to pose for a portrait. He then carefully poses the volunteer, and when satisfied with the pose, he holds to his eye a spoon, as if it were a candid camera, and focuses it on the

191

person to be photographed. He may say, "Now, smile please" or "Look at the birdie." Then he makes a clicking sound, and the picture is taken.

After this little act, the photographer calls back his confederate and, without saying a word, hands him the spoon, and sits down. The confederate studies the spoon intently, looks around the room, and immediately points out the person who posed for the picture.

It is all very simple. When the photographer sits down, after turning over the spoon to his confederate, he assumes the same position as that of the person who has been photographed. (Obviously, if the subject of the portrait should be standing, the photographer will have to stand in a like manner.) After looking at the photographer, it is an easy matter for the confederate to identify the subject.

125. Tongue-Twisters

Two tired tadpoles tippling tea.

Five frightfully frightened frogs frantically fleeing flames.

Ten timid tinsmiths tinning tanks.

She sells sea shells by the seashore.

She swore she never saw the sea so calm before.

Six thick thistle sticks.

Peter Piper picked a peck of pickled peppers.

Mary Mixer mixed biscuits Monday.